P9-CMT-646

BICYCLE
REPAIR
MANUAL

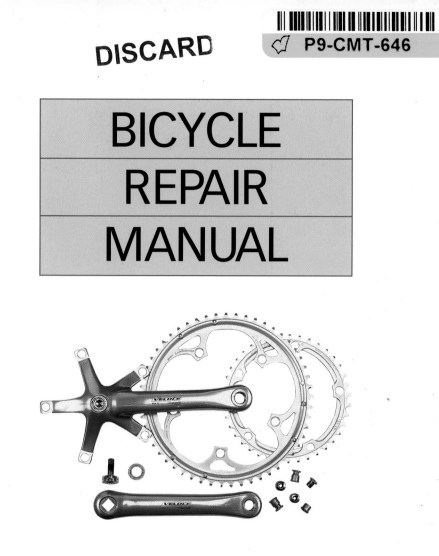

BICYCLE
REPAIR
MANUAL

CHRIS SIDWELLS

LONDON, NEW YORK, MUNICH,
MELBOURNE, AND DELHI

Senior Editor Richard Gilbert
Senior Art Editor Susan St. Louis
Managing Editor Stephanie Farrow
Managing Art Editor Lee Griffiths
Jacket Designer Lee Ellwood

Senior Production Editor Vânia Cunha
Production Controller Louise Daly

Produced for Dorling Kindersley by
Editor Pip Morgan
Designer Peter Laws

Original edition designed by
Edward Kinsey

Photographer Gerard Brown
Technical Consultant Guy Andrews

First American Edition 2004. Published with minor
revisions in 2005, this edition fully revised and
updated in 2008 in the United States by
DK Publishing, 375 Hudson Street
New York, New York 10014

08 09 10 11   10 9 8 7 6 5 4 3 2 1

BD588–06/08

Published in Great Britain by Dorling Kindersley
Limited.

A catalog record for this book is available from the
Library of Congress.

ISBN 978-0-75663-394-3

DK books are available at special discounts when
purchased in bulk for sales promotions, premiums,
fund-raising, or educational use. For details, contact:
DK Publishing Special Markets, 375 Hudson Street,
New York, New York 10014 or SpecialSales@dk.com.

Color reproduction by Colourscan in Singapore
Printed and bound by Star Standard
in Singapore

Discover more at
www.dk.com

Contents

Introduction

A clean, well-maintained bike will work efficiently and safely, and add to your enjoyment of cycling by giving you peace of mind.

Safety and efficiency are closely linked. If your gears are not shifting correctly, for instance, they will not only affect your riding efficiency, but also tempt you to look down at them while riding to see what is causing the problem. As a result, you might take your eyes off what is happening on the road ahead and expose yourself to the possibility of a collision. The *Bicycle Repair Manual* will help you avoid such problems by demonstrating how to maintain your bike regularly and correctly.

Understanding technology

Modern bikes may seem complicated, and the technology that manufacturers use may be more sophisticated than ever. However, cycle components work, as they always have, according to logical principles, so there is no reason for you to be daunted.

Before you begin to service a particular component of your bike, first become familiar with the part by turning to the relevant section. Knowing how a part works makes it easier to maintain.

Above all, be confident and patient with what you are doing. Even if you do not think of yourself as mechanically minded, you may come to enjoy bike maintenance after a while and will certainly enjoy the trouble-free cycling that rewards your efforts.

Collecting information

If you buy a new bike, make sure that you keep the accompanying owner's manual, so that you can refer to it alongside this book. Do the same with any new equipment that you buy.

If your bike is not new, obtain a manual from a bike shop or the manufacturer's Web site. Manuals will help you to be aware of the particular maintenance requirements of all the components on your bike.

If you want to learn more about bike mechanics, there are many magazines available that contain tips on specific components. However, the large majority of people who are simply interested in learning how to maintain their bike will find everything they need to know in the pages of the *Bicycle Repair Manual*.

Using this book

The different maintenance requirements of the most common types of bikes are listed at the beginning of the book. These requirements are covered in the step-by-step pages that are specific to the components fitted to each type of bike—for example, suspension forks for mountain bikes.

You will also find a timetable for servicing the parts of your bike and a troubleshooting chart to help you identify and solve problems. The book helps you to spot danger signs and to carry out routine safety checks. These features detail what you need to do and refer you to the relevant step-by-step sequences to explain how to do it.

GETTING TO

Understanding your bike
will make it easier to
maintain. Identify all the
different parts and
components to help you
see how they work
together as a whole.

KNOW YOUR BIKE

The basic bike

Modern bikes, such as the hybrid bike (*below*), are designed to be light and user-friendly. Each part performs a key function in the overall operation of the bike.

The frame is the skeleton on to which all components are fitted. The fork holds the front wheel, and connects to the handlebars so the bike can be steered. Suspension forks improve comfort and control over rough surfaces. The drivetrain is the system that transfers the rider's energy, via the pedals and cranks, to the rear wheel. It also contains a number of cogs, known as chainrings and cogs, which carry the chain.

The derailleurs change the bike's gears by moving the chain onto different chainrings and cogs. Derailleurs are controlled by the gear-shift levers, which are mounted on the handlebar to allow quick and easy use by the rider. The brakes are controlled by brake

Hybrid bike ▶
Advances in technology have refined the design and improved the performance of each category of bike part, producing a machine that is easy to ride and maintain.

Wheel (*see pp.98–9, 102–7*)
The rim's shape and high-tech aluminum increase the wheel's strength. Wheels with disc brakes, shown here, can have lighter rims than bikes with rim brakes.

Derailleur (*see pp.50–5*)
Derailleurs are designed to cope with the wide range of sprocket sizes required to climb and descend the steepest hills.

Frame (*see pp.12–13*)
Improved welding techniques allow thin-walled aluminum tubes to provide a relatively cheap, light and responsive frame. The thickness of the tube walls varies to cope with areas of increased stress.

Pedal (*see pp.78–85*)
Clipless pedals allow more power to be transferred to the wheels because the feet are fixed to the pedals. Flat pedals, and toe clips and straps, are simpler, but easier to use.

Drivetrain (*see pp.56–77*)
Stiff materials maximize the amount of power the drivetrain transfers to the rear wheel. A triple crankset increases gear range and a flexible chain allows quick, easy gear-shifts.

levers that are also mounted on the handle-bar, and use brake pads to press against the wheel's rim, or discs attached to the hub, to stop the bike.

High-tech machine ▶
Many years of design refinement have produced an adaptable hybrid bike, which combines technology from road and mountain bikes for use in an urban environment.

Gear-shift levers
(*see pp.44–9*)
Ergonomically designed gear-shift levers were developed from mountain bikes, and give easy, precise gear-shifts.

Fork (*see pp.138–47*)
Forks are designed with varying thickness in the tube wall. Tubes are thin in the middle and thick at both ends. This reduces weight and absorbs road shock. Some forks also act as suspension systems, further reducing shock and improving control.

Brake (*see pp.108–35*)
Disc brakes offer sensitive, powerful braking that is not affected by weather conditions. Other bikes have rim brakes, which are still very good, although they require earlier braking to slow in the wet.

Tire (*see pp.104–5*)
Modern tires are made from rubber compounds that roll well on the road, while adhering to it when cornering. They often have puncture-resistant bands of material, such as Kevlar, beneath the tread.

Anatomy of the bike

Understanding how the parts on your bike fit together will help you perform maintenance tasks successfully. Although your bike may differ from the modern mountain bike (*right*), all bikes fit together in a similar way. For example, the quick-release levers on the wheels below perform the same function as axle nuts on a bike with hub gears.

   The main parts and their components, and where each part is attached to the bike, are shown on the mountain bike. Take the time to study the illustration, since it will act as a useful reference to help you follow the steps later in the book.

Mountain bike ▶
The mountain bike is a good example of how parts fit together—its frame, wheels, drivetrain, pedals, derailleurs, brakes, and gear-shift levers are similar to those of road and hybrid bikes.

Saddle
Saddle cover
Saddle rails

Seat post
Saddle clamp

Rear brake
Cable-guide tube
Braking surface
Brake pad
Brake arm

Frame
Seat tube
Seat stay
Chainstay
Down tube

Rear hub
Rear dropout
Hub
Quick-release

Bottom bracket

Cassette
Cassette body
Cog
Lockring

Rear derailleur
Jockey pulley
Derailleur plate
Barrel adjuster

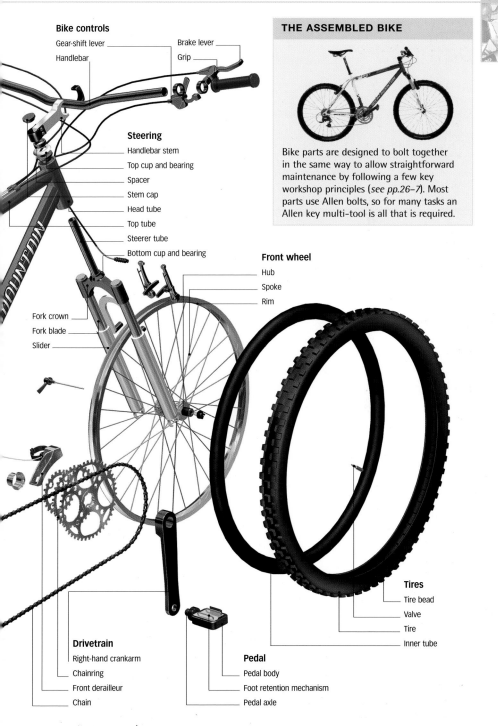

Bike controls

Gear-shift lever

Handlebar

Brake lever

Grip

THE ASSEMBLED BIKE

Bike parts are designed to bolt together in the same way to allow straightforward maintenance by following a few key workshop principles (*see pp.26–7*). Most parts use Allen bolts, so for many tasks an Allen key multi-tool is all that is required.

Steering

Handlebar stem

Top cup and bearing

Spacer

Stem cap

Head tube

Top tube

Steerer tube

Bottom cup and bearing

Front wheel

Hub

Spoke

Rim

Fork crown

Fork blade

Slider

Tires

Tire bead

Valve

Tire

Inner tube

Drivetrain

Right-hand crankarm

Chainring

Front derailleur

Chain

Pedal

Pedal body

Foot retention mechanism

Pedal axle

Bikes for general use

You can buy a bike for almost any purpose, but even a simple utility, hybrid, or folding bike will still increase your fitness, save you money on train or bus tickets, and have no negative impact on your environment.

As long as the bike is of good quality, you will only need to keep it clean and check it regularly for signs of wear. Hybrid bikes, utility bikes, and folding bikes are all dependable machines that are suitable for commuting to work or school, day-to-day transportation, or simply a relaxing ride on a bike trail or country road.

The hybrid bike

Lightweight materials combined with road-bike performance and hardy mountain bike technology make hybrid bikes perfect for bumpy urban roads. They are ideal for commuting, family rides, fitness riding, touring, and carrying luggage.

The utility bike

Utility bikes are ideal for local commuting and short rides. They are equipped with fat tires that absorb road bumps but will drag on long journeys, making them tiring and uncomfortable to ride.

The folding bike

Ideal for commuters, and for people with little space in which to store a standard bike, folding bikes can go anywhere, especially on public transportation. The folded bike can be easily reassembled into a serviceable machine without the use of tools.

Urban commuting
With its head-up, traffic-friendly riding position and easy-to-operate gears, the lightweight hybrid is ideal for urban commuting.

ESSENTIAL MAINTENANCE CHECKLIST
HYBRID BIKE

- Regularly maintain and lubricate the derailleur gears (see *pp.52–3, 54–5*).
- Check the gear cables for signs of wear (see *p.39, pp.48–9*).
- Check the brake cables or hoses, and pads for signs of wear (see *p.39, pp.114–15*).
- Check the tires for signs of wear (see *p.39*).
- Regularly change the chain (see *pp.64–5*).

Tire — Rear derailleur — Front derailleur — Gear cable — Brake cable — Chain

UTILITY BIKE

- Regularly lubricate the hub gears (see *pp.58–9, 60–1*).
- Regularly check the gear cables for signs of wear (see *p.39*).
- Regularly check the brake control cables for signs of wear (*pp.114–15*).
- Regularly check the brake pads for signs of wear (see *p.38*).
- Regularly clean and grease the chain (see *pp.28–9, 30–1*).

Sprung saddle — Brake lever — Handlebar basket — Hub gears — Chainguard

FOLDING BIKE

- Regularly check and lubricate the pivots and the locks that allow the bike to fold and unfold.
- Regularly check hub gears, even though they are shielded from the elements and so need very little maintenance (see *pp.58–9, 60–1*)
- Pay extra attention to the outer control cables (see *p.39, pp.48–9*).

Rear suspension — Hub and derailleur gear system — Frame hinge — Large chainrings — Folded bike — Unfolded bike

Specialty bikes

If you want to take up cycling as a sport or hobby, rather than simply as a means of transportation, look for a more specialized bike, such as a race-level road bike, a mountain bike, or a BMX bike.

As bikes become more sophisticated, they need more care. For example, lightweight parts wear quickly, so they must be kept scrupulously clean. Carbon wheel rims require special brake pads that do not work well on metal. Hydraulic disc brakes and suspension systems need regular attention.

Do not let this stop you from buying your dream bike. Just as riding it will be a joy, maintaining it to exacting standards will be part of the whole cycling experience.

The road bike
Lightweight materials and narrow tires make road bikes good for fitness riding, day touring, and competitions. The aerodynamic position afforded by a drop handlebar offers great speed. Road bikes are so light and have such a range of gears that almost anyone, with a little training, can tackle the great mountain passes made famous by the Tour de France.

The mountain bike
Full-suspension mountain bikes allow you to break new ground and ride across rugged terrain that was previously unthinkable and at speeds that were once unattainable.

The BMX bike
These bikes are built for acceleration and agile bike handling. Like some of the very first bikes, BMXs are made almost entirely from steel because it transfers power in a way that no other material can.

Road riding
This road bike represents the ultimate in road-bike design, and is the type of bike that professionals use in the Tour de France.

ESSENTIAL MAINTENANCE CHECKLIST

ROAD BIKE

- Regularly clean and lubricate the bike (see pp.28–9, 30–1).
- Make routine safety checks (see pp.32–3).
- Check the brakes (see pp.116–17).
- Make sure gears are working perfectly (see pp.52–3, 54–5).
- Check frame protector pads for wear in the locations where cable outers touch carbon-fiber frames (see p.33).

Caliper brake

20-speed gear-shift system

Carbon-fiber frame

Aluminum drop handlebar

Road race tire

Clipless pedal

Deep section carbon fiber rims

MOUNTAIN BIKE

- Set up the suspension system (see pp.140-1, 150–1).
- Regularly clean and lubricate the suspension (see pp.142–3, 144–5).
- Inspect all pivots and seals regularly.
- Check brake cables or hoses, and pads regularly (see pp.38–9, pp.114–15).
- Replace the cassette every six months (see pp.66–7).
- Service the headset regularly (see pp.90–1, 92–3).

Rear shock

Rear derailleur

Carbon-fiber frame

Straight handlebar

Cross-country tire

Suspension fork

Disc brake

BMX BIKE

- Regularly check the bottom bracket to see that it is running free, but not loose (see pp.76–7).
- Replace the pedals if their axles are bent (see pp.80–1).
- Adjust the brakes for minimal travel before the brakes come on, since the steel rims, though very strong, do not make good braking surfaces (see pp.122–3).

Single gearing

Gyro headset

Stunt peg

Opposite transmission

Setting up an adult's bike

If the saddle's height and angle are adjusted and the position of the brake levers on the handlebar is set so that they are within easy reach, then riding will be more efficient and comfortable. A novice cyclist should try setting the saddle height a little lower at first, and work toward the ideal once he or she is used to riding.

STEP LOCATOR

Toolbox

- Allen key multi-tool ● Wrenches
- Screwdriver

Adjusting your riding position

1 **Remove your shoes** and sit on your bike, supporting yourself against a wall.

- Set your crankarms so that the pedal farthest from the wall is at the low point of its revolution.
- Put the heel of your foot on the pedal. Your leg should be straight when you do this. Ask someone to help you check.

The knee aligns with the axle

4 **Place the widest part** of your foot over the pedal axle. If your shoes have cleats, set them up so that your foot can easily adopt this position (see pp.84–5).

- Set your crankarms parallel to the floor. The depression on the side of your leading leg, just behind the kneecap, should be directly over the axle of the pedal. Ask your helper to check.

5 **Move your saddle back** if the depression on your leg is in front of the axle. If it is behind, move it forward.

- Undo the saddle clamp under the saddle. On modern bikes, you will need an Allen key; on older bikes, use a wrench.
- Repeat Steps 4 and 5 until you are sure you have the position right.

2 Raise the saddle if your leg is not straight when your heel is on the pedal. Lower the saddle if your heel does not reach the pedal.

● Undo the seat pin clamp bolt. Raise or lower the saddle, tighten up the bolt, and try again. Ask your helper to see if your leg is straight. Do not lean on the foot that you are testing.

3 To make absolutely sure the saddle height is right for you, go for a ride with your cycling shoes on and your feet in their normal position on the pedals.

● Ask your helper to ride behind you and make sure your hips are not rocking from side to side as you ride. If they are, the saddle is set too high and you need to repeat Steps 1 and 2.

6 Make sure that the brake reach allows you to apply the brakes using the first joints of your first two fingers, while holding the handlebar securely with your thumb and remaining fingers. You should be able to hook your fingers over the brake levers. If you have to stretch too far, you will be unable to apply enough power.

7 Adjust the reach of the brake levers if you have to stretch too far.

● Undo the brake cable (*see pp.118–19*) and screw in the adjuster on the lever until you can reach it easily. Then reclamp the brake cables.

● Set the brake levers at an angle to the handlebar so that you can pull them in line with your arm.

Setting up a child's bike

Before a child starts riding a bike, adjust the saddle and handlebar to suit his or her body. Set the saddle at its lowest point, as in Step 1. Buy the biggest bike possible at first, then keep adjusting it as the child grows taller. Children's bikes are usually measured by wheel size—from 12in (30cm) up to 24in (60cm).

STEP LOCATOR

Toolbox
- Allen key multi-tool ● Wrenches
- Plastic mallet

Adjusting the position of the saddle

1 **Set the saddle** on your child's bike at a height that allows him or her to sit on it and simultaneously to touch the ground with the front part of each foot. This is the ideal setup.

Adjusting the height of the handlebar

1 **Raise or lower the bike's handlebar** by loosening the expander bolt that holds the stem into the bike. This bolt is secured by either an Allen bolt or a hexagonal bolt, so use an Allen key or a wrench to loosen it.

● Knock the bolt down with a plastic mallet to free it up if you need to.

2 **Grip the front wheel** between your legs to steady it and then pull the handlebar up or push it down. Do not pull the handlebar higher than the safety limit that is marked on the stem. Once the handlebar is at the right height, and the stem is lined up with the front wheel, tighten the expander bolt.

2 **Loosen the seat pin clamp**—it has either a quick-release lever or a nut-and-bolt fixing that requires a wrench. Either pull the saddle up or push it down to the required height.

3 **Move the saddle** forward or backward by loosening the nut that secures the seat clamp. Tighten the nut again, but be sure that the saddle is horizontal to the ground.

3 **Adjust the saddle** and handlebar still further if you need to, so that your child can sit in the ideal riding position— neither too upright, nor too stretched.

CARING FOR YOUR BIKE

Your bike needs to be kept clean and well lubricated to avoid mechanical problems. Learning to make cleaning, lubricating, and checking a regular part of your bike routine will lengthen the life of your bike and its components.

Tools

If you are going to regularly maintain and repair your bike, you will need to buy a tool kit or assemble your own. The tools shown opposite will enable you to carry out all the essential repairs and to maintain your bike at peak performance. Add other tools as required when specific parts of your bike need maintenance or replacement. However, try to follow a few general principles when using the tools.

When using tools on a bike, especially lightweight bikes, you need a delicate touch. If you are used to working on cars, then use less force when dealing with your bike. Nuts and bolts only need to be tight; if you over-tighten them, they will shear. If in doubt, buy torque gauges that accurately measure the correct level of tightness on a bike's nuts and bolts. See the component manufacturers' instructions for recommended torque settings. In fact, it is essential to keep all the instructions that come with your bike, tools, and any components you buy.

Buy the best-quality, precision-made tools. They will last for many years if you take care of them. Cheap tools will bend and become chipped, making it impossible to carry out some maintenance jobs properly. They could even damage the components that you work on.

Working with tools
When using your tools to maintain or repair your bike, give yourself plenty of room and always work in a neat, well-lit environment.

Essential tools

Start your toolbox with the two multi-tools, the wrenches to fit the cones, needle-nose pliers, cable cutters, a pump, and a workstand.

Pumps and Workstand

Wrenches and Allen Keys

Drivetrain Tools

Bottom Bracket Tools

Mallet

Pliers and Cable Cutters

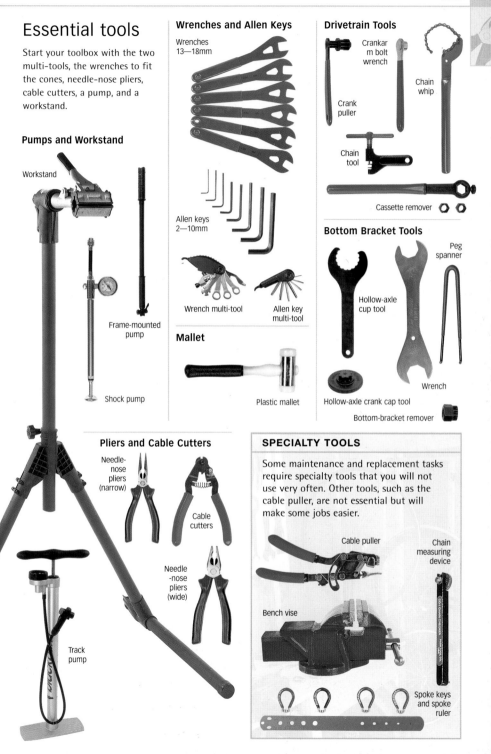

Workstand

Frame-mounted pump

Shock pump

Track pump

Wrenches 13—18mm

Allen keys 2—10mm

Wrench multi-tool

Allen key multi-tool

Plastic mallet

Needle-nose pliers (narrow)

Cable cutters

Needle-nose pliers (wide)

Crankar m bolt wrench

Crank puller

Chain tool

Chain whip

Cassette remover

Peg spanner

Hollow-axle cup tool

Wrench

Hollow-axle crank cap tool

Bottom-bracket remover

SPECIALTY TOOLS

Some maintenance and replacement tasks require specialty tools that you will not use very often. Other tools, such as the cable puller, are not essential but will make some jobs easier.

Cable puller

Chain measuring device

Bench vise

Spoke keys and spoke ruler

Workshop principles

Four key principles govern the work you do on your bike. The first is neatness—find a place for each tool and return it there when you are finished with it. Second, do not use too much force to tighten components—the nuts and bolts of lightweight parts can easily shear. Third, remember the order in which you take components apart. Finally, keep all of your tools clean and dry.

The guidelines below provide you with general principles for some of the most common tools or operations in bike repair.

Using Allen keys

Put the long axis of an Allen key in the Allen bolt to make the key easier to use, both for repeated turns and in places where space is tight or restricted, such as putting a bottle cage on the down tube.

Use the short axis of an Allen key to make the final turn when tightening an Allen bolt—for example, on a chainring. You can also use this technique to start undoing an Allen bolt.

Using pliers

Use needle-nose pliers to hold cables and keep them under tension. Buy a small pair with pointed jaws for tight areas. Keep the jaws clean and grease-free. Lubricate the pivot with light oil occasionally.

Fix a cable crimp onto a brake cable to stop the ends from fraying. Push the cable crimp onto the end of the cable and squeeze it flat with your pliers. If you are gentle, you can use the inside jaws of your cable cutters.

Using a wrench

Always use the correct size of wrench for the nut you are tightening or loosening. Hold the wrench firmly at the end to maximize leverage. Make sure that the jaws fully enclose the nut to prevent it from slipping.

Cutting cable housings

Cut a brake cable housing between the spirals of the metal tube under the sheath. If the spirals become compressed, squeeze them with the inside of your cutter jaws until they are round.

Cut a gear cable housing through the wire under the sheath. If you need to, squeeze the wire with the inside of your cutter jaws until its cross-section is round again.

Organizing a bike workshop
Regularly maintaining your bike and carrying
out essential repairs means that you can keep
your bike at peak performance. If you have the
space, the best place to do this is in a workshop
that is well organized and equipped with all the
tools you need for your particular bike. Create a
workshop that is dry with plenty of light—and
follow the four key workshop principles.

Cleaning your bike

Although a bike is a very efficient and durable machine, some of its more delicate parts are at the mercy of the elements. Grit and dirt, for example, stick to lubricants and act as a grinding agent. Clean the parts regularly to keep them running smoothly and prevent them from wearing out.

While cleaning your bike, check all the parts and components for damage. With the wheels taken out, you can look at parts of the bike's frame that are usually hidden and examine each component for signs of dangerous wear (see pp.32–3 and pp.38–9).

The process of cleaning is straightforward. First, remove old lubricants by applying a degreaser. Then wash the dirt off with water and detergent. Finally, rinse, dry, and lubricate the exposed moving parts.

Cleaning equipment

- Plastic bucket ● Sponges ● Degreaser ● Cloth
- Hard-bristled brushes ● Cassette scraper

Removing dirt and oil

1 **Remove both wheels** from the bike and put the frame in a workstand or hang it up.

- Place a chain holder in the rear dropout to keep the chain tight while the rear wheel is out of the bike. This allows the chain to run freely so that it can be cleaned thoroughly.

- Apply a degreaser to remove any old oil and grit. Spray onto the crankset, the front and rear derailleurs, and the chain, covering each link.

4 **Clean the rest of the wheel,** including the tires, with a bigger brush and soapy water.

- Work the bristles in between the spokes and around the hub. Rinse with clean water and dry everything with a cloth.

5 **Spray the chainrings,** crankset, and front derailleur with more degreaser if there is still stubborn oil and dirt (inset).

- Dip the sponge in hot, soapy water and wrap it around the chain. Turn the pedals so the chain runs through the sponge.

- Use the same sponge to wash the rear derailleur, the front derailleur, and the chainrings.

2 **Use a cassette scraper** to gouge out any dirt and debris that has accumulated between the cogs.

3 **Use a hard-bristled brush** on the cassette so that the degreaser reaches into the spaces between the cogs. Allow a few minutes for the degreaser to work, and wash it off with soapy water.

6 **Apply plenty of soapy water** to the rest of the bike with a different sponge. Start at the top and work down.

● Use different-sized, hard-bristled brushes to work the water into the places that are hard to reach.

● Rinse with clean water and dry the bike with a clean cloth.

● Use a sponge to work soap into intricate parts, such as between the brake arms and the pads.

● Replace the wheels and sparingly apply a light oil to the chain and the moving parts of the front and rear derailleurs.

Lubricating your bike

Regular lubrication helps a bike to run smoothly and prevents excessive wear and tear. Each time a part of the bike is lubricated, remember to remove the old oil and grease with degreaser first (*see pp.28–9*). Applying new lubrication on top of old does not work because lubricants attract grit and dirt to the bike and form a grinding paste that can cause damage.

The lubricants needed vary from light spray oil (dry lube) and heavier oil (wet lube) to light grease manufactured specifically for bikes and anti-seize compounds.

STEP LOCATOR

Applying oil and grease

1 **Dribble some light oil** inside the cable housings before you fit a new cable. This makes sure that the cable runs smoothly inside. Poor gear-shifts are often due to cables running dry inside their housings. The same is true of brakes that are hard to apply and slow to return to the ready-to-use position.

3 **Dribble light oil** on to the pivots in the front and rear derailleurs once a week. The jockey pulleys on the rear derailleur also need some light oil where they rotate around the jockey pulley bolts.

● Make sure you flush out any old oil with degreaser first.

4 **Oil the chain** after riding in wet weather, and clean, dry, and lubricate when cleaning your bike (*see pp.28–9*). Except in winter, or in bad conditions, use light oil from a spray can or bottle.

● Hold a cloth underneath the chain to catch any excess oil.

5 **Grease open bearings** after regular cleaning with a light grease specifically made for bikes. Bottom brackets and hubs need most attention, but headsets need regreasing less often. Riding regularly in the rain shortens the interval between lubrications.

2 Smear grease on all new cables and, occasionally, on old ones.

- Place a blob of grease on the nipple end of the cable, then pull the cable through your thumb and index finger before fitting it. Wear mechanic's disposable gloves.

 Spread anti-seize compound on the seat pin and stem to prevent the two components from binding with the seat tube or steerer tube. Although you can use grease in place of anti-seize, always use a copper-based anti-seize compound for lubricating components made with carbon fiber.

Making routine safety checks

Every week or so, check the bike frame for signs of wear. Before going for a ride, run through a few checks to reduce the chances of a mechanical failure: brakes that cease to work, a loose handlebar, a tire blowout, or slipping gears. The checks will help to avoid many of the accidents caused by equipment failures. Safety checks help the management of a bike, allowing the timely replacement of parts or the completion of non-urgent maintenance work.

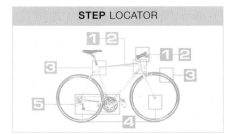

STEP LOCATOR

Making frame checks

1 **Inspect the frame** every week or so and look for metal fatigue. Run a finger under the down tube where it joins the head tube. A ripple in the tube's surface could lead to a break.

● Check around the area where the chainstay bridge is brazed to the chainstays, particularly on a steel frame. Cracks may form in the metal here because of the heat of the brazing process.

Making pre-ride checks

1 **Hold the front wheel** firmly between your legs and try to turn the handlebar from one side to the other. If there is any movement, check the stem and steerer bolts and tighten them if necessary.

● Try twisting the bar upward to look for rotational movement.

2 **Apply each brake** fully and push the bike forward. If the lever pulls to the bar before the brake stops a wheel from rotating, adjust the travel or replace the pads.

● Apply the front brake. Tighten the headset if you feel any play in the steerer assembly.

3 **Lift the bike,** slowly spin the wheels, and check the tires for cuts, splits, or bulges. If you find a bulge, or are in any doubt, replace the tire. Check the tire pressure.

● Remove anything stuck in the tire, as it may cause the tire to deflate (see pp.104–5).

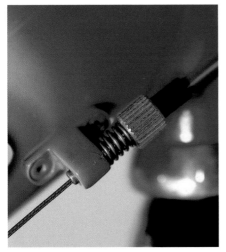

2 **Monitor all the parts** that are riveted to an aluminum frame, especially the cable guides or the front derailleur hangers. The rivets form potentially weak areas where stresses in the metal may develop into cracks.

3 **Protect carbon-fiber frames** in areas where the cable outers touch them. Buy a self-adhesive protective patch and peel off the back. Place it on the frame, sticky side down, under the cable outer—it is very important to prevent the cable from wearing down the carbon frame. Check the patches regularly and replace them when worn.

4 **Check that all quick-release** levers are in the locked position, and wheel nuts are tight. Look for the words "lock" and "unlock" on the levers— "lock" is outermost when the wheel is secure (*see pp. 102–3*).

5 **Run through the gears** and make sure that they are properly adjusted. Gears that will not mesh properly after you change them can be distracting and, if you look down to see what is wrong, potentially dangerous. If the gears are correctly adjusted and the chain is still jumping, check for a stiff link.

Maintenance

Schedule the work you need to carry out on your bike by developing a maintenance timetable. The timetable on the right provides a good template, since it shows the tasks you should perform on your bike and suggests when you should do them.

Your schedule depends on how much and where your bike is ridden. A heavily used off-road bike requires attention at much shorter intervals, while a bike used for infrequent, short road journeys will need less regular attention.

However, work carried out as part of a maintenance schedule does not replace the safety checks that must be carried out before every ride (*see pp.32–3*), or regularly looking for danger signs (*see pp.38–9*). You should also check your bike and lubricate the drivetrain every time you clean it.

MAINTENANCE TIMETABLE

EVERY WEEK

DRIVETRAIN	CHECK	Chain for wear (*see pp.64–5*) Gear-shift performance (*see pp.46–9, 52–5*) Inner cables for fraying and outer cables for wear (*see pp.46–9*) Crankarms and chainring bolts for tightness (*see pp.68–9*)
	LUBRICATE	Oil chain (*see pp.30–1*) Oil jockey pulleys (*see pp.54–5*)
	REPLACE	
STEERING AND WHEELS	CHECK	Headset for looseness and ease of steering (*see pp.90–3*) Action of quick-release levers (*see pp.102–3*) Wheels for broken spokes and trueness (*see pp.106–7*) Handlebar and stem for cracks (*see pp.94–7*)
	LUBRICATE	
	REPLACE	
BRAKES	CHECK	Inner cables for fraying and and outer cables for wear (*see pp.112–15*) Pads for wear and alignment (*see pp.116–3, 128–9*) Hydraulic hoses for wear, kinks, or leaks (*see pp.130–1*) Brake levers, arms, discs, and calipers for cracks (*see pp.112–23, pp.128–33*) Disc and caliper bolts for tightness (*see pp.130–1*)
	LUBRICATE	Oil exposed cables by wiping with wet lube on a rag
	REPLACE	
SUSPENSION	CHECK	Fork and shock exterior surfaces for cracks (*see pp.142–45, 150–51*) Stanchions under shock boots, if fitted, for cracks (*see pp.140–1*) Top caps, crown bolts, and shaft bolts for tightness (*see pp.138–9, 142–3, 144–5*)
	LUBRICATE	Teflon oil on fork stanchions and shock body, and on all seals (*see pp.140–47, 150–1*)
	REPLACE	

EVERY MONTH

Bottom bracket for smooth running, play, and bent axle (see pp.72–7)
Pedals for play, and clipless pedals for play and release action (see pp.80–3)
Rear derailleur pivots for play (see pp.54–5)
Cog and chainring teeth for wear (see pp.66–9)

Oil derailleur pivots (see pp.30–1)
Oil and grease inner and outer cables (see pp.30–1)
Oil clipless pedal release mechanisms (see pp.40–1)

Chain on a heavily used bike (see pp.40–1, 64–5)

Hubs for play on axles, roughness, or tight spots (see pp.100–3)
Rubber seals on hubs for splits (see pp.100–3)
Covers, if fitted, on headsets (see pp.40–1)

Oil the seals on hubs (see pp.100–3)

Discs for wear and calipers for alignment (see pp.130–1)

Grease inner cables and oil inside outer cables (see pp.30–1, 114–17)

Brake pads of heavily used mountain bikes (see pp.120–23)

Fork and shock for play (see pp.140–5, 150–1)
Fork stanchions to see if oil line visible (see pp.140–5)
Fork and shock seals for cracks and slackness (see pp.140–5, 150–1).
(Play, absence of oil lines, and cracked seals are all evidence of worn seals, which should be replaced by a trained technician.)
Fork and shock sag (see pp.140–1, 150–1)

Turn bike upside down and store overnight so oil can redistribute in fork

EVERY SIX MONTHS

Freehub body and freewheel for play (see pp.66–7)
Rear derailleur frame fixing bolt for play (see pp.54–5)
Cleats for wear (see pp.84–5)
Jockey pulleys for wear (see pp.54–5)

Oil in hub gear, if equipped with oil port (see pp.58–9)
Grease bearings in pedals (see pp.80–1)

Chain (see pp.64–5)
Inner and outer cables (see pp.46–9)
Cogs on a heavily used bike (see pp.66–7)

Bearings in open-bearing hubs for wear (see pp.100–1)
Bearings and bearing surfaces in headsets for wear (see pp.90–3)

Grease open-bearing hubs (see pp.100–1)
Grease headsets (see pp.90–3)

Handlebar tape and grips (see pp.94–7)

Grease brake bosses (see pp.120–1)

Inner and outer cables (see pp.112–15)

Fork steerer for cracks, by removing the headset (see pp.90–3)

Fork oil (see pp.142–5)
Seals on forks and shocks, as part of biannual service by trained technician

Troubleshooting

The symptoms of some of the things that can go wrong with your bike are listed in this troubleshooting chart. It explains why a bike may be showing these symptoms and then suggests a solution, referring you to the pages where you will find a detailed sequence of steps to guide you.

If you still find the problem difficult to solve, consult the How They Work pages for the specific part you are working on, so that you can understand it better. However, sometimes the symptoms confronting you can be due to a malfunction other than the one suggested in this chart. If, after consulting the relevant pages in the book, you still cannot solve the problem, ask the experts at a good bike shop for help.

SOLVING COMMON PROBLEM

PROBLEM

DRIVETRAIN

The chain will not shift onto a smaller cog or chainring.

The chain will not shift onto a larger cog or it shifts but does not run smoothly on it.

The chain shifts cleanly, but jumps on the cogs when pressure is applied to the pedals.

The chain rubs on the inner then the outer side of the front derailleur cage. On a bike with a single chainring, the chain persistently falls off.

STEERING AND WHEELS

When you apply the front brake and push the bike forward, the headset moves forward relative to the head tube.

You hear a sudden snapping noise come from a wheel while riding and/or the wheel goes out of true.

There is side-to-side play of a hub on its axle, or when turning the axle in the hub you feel either a roughness or tight and loose spots.

When pedalling forward, the cassette spins, but there is no drive to the bike. Alternatively, the cassette spins before the drive is engaged or there is much side-to-side play in the cassette.

BRAKES

The brakes are hard to apply, and/or sluggish to release.

You have to pull the brake lever a long way before the brakes engage.

The two brake pads do not contact the braking surface at the same time.

The brake pads contact the braking surface without pulling the lever too far, but are ineffective at slowing the bike.

SUSPENSION

The fork regularly reaches the limit of its travel (bottoms out).

On steep, smooth descents, the rear wheel lifts under braking.

The front wheel judders up and down when cornering.

A rear air/oil shock regularly reaches the limit of its travel (bottoms out).

CAUSE	SOLUTION
Either grit has become lodged inside the cable housing or the cable lubrication has dried up.	Strip down the cables, flush the housings with degreaser, clean the inners with degreaser, lubricate, and reassemble. (*See pp.30–1, 46–9*)
The cable has stretched or the relevant derailleur is poorly adjusted.	Unclamp the cable at the derailleur, pull through any slack, and retighten. Then set up the derailleur. (*See pp.52–5*)
Either the chain has a stiff link; or the chain or cogs, or both, are worn; or a chainring may be bent	Check the chain for a stiff link and remove it if found. If no stiff link is found, replace the chain. If the problem persists, replace the cogs. If the chainring is bent, replace it. (*See pp.62–9*)
The bottom bracket is worn or its axle may be bent.	If the bottom bracket is a cartridge type, replace it. If it is a hollow-axle bottom bracket, replace the cup and bearing units. If it is a BMX bottom bracket, it may be possible to replace the bearings if they are worn, or to replace the axle if it is bent. (*See pp.72–7*)
The headset is loose or worn.	Strip and inspect the headset. Replace bearings if worn, regrease, and reassemble. Inspect the cups and races; if they are worn you should let a good bike shop replace the whole headset. (*See pp.90–3*)
A spoke may have broken.	Replace the spoke and true the wheel. (*See pp.106–7*)
The hub bearings are worn or, in the case of tight and loose spots, the axle is bent.	Replace the bearings or the axle. (*See pp.100–1*)
The freehub body is worn.	Replace the freehub body. (*See pp.100–1*)
Grit and dirt is inside the cable housing or the lubrication on the inner cables has dried up.	Strip down the cables, flush the housings, and clean the inner cables with degreaser, lubricate both, and reassemble. (*See pp.30–1, 112–15*)
The pads are wearing down or the cable has slipped through the clamp bolt.	If the pads are not too worn, take up the extra travel by unclamping the brakes, pulling the cable through the clamp, and tightening. If the pads are worn, replace them. (*See pp.110–23, 126–35*)
Your brakes are not centered.	Follow the procedures for centering the type of brakes on your bike. (*See pp.110–23, 128–35*)
There is grease on the pads, foreign objects are embedded in them, or they are wearing unevenly. You may even need a different compound of brake pad.	Rub the pads with emery cloth. Remove foreign bodies with needle-nose pliers. Fit new pads if they are worn unevenly. Seek advice from a bike shop regarding different pad compounds. (*See pp.110–23, 126–35*)
With air/oil forks, not enough air is in the system. With coil/oil forks, too light a spring is fitted.	Pump in more air. Replace springs with heavier-duty springs. (*See pp.140–3*)
The front of the bike is diving under braking because the fork is not stiff enough.	Pump in air, or increase preload, according to the type of fork on your bike. (*See pp.140–3*)
The fork's rebound is set too fast.	Use the relevant adjuster to reduce the speed of the fork's rebound. (*See pp.140–3*)
Insufficient air in the shock, or too much damping, means that the shock is not returning from each compression quickly enough.	Set up the sag on the shock again. If the problem continues, use the damping adjustment to speed up the action of the shock. (*See pp.150–1*)

Spotting danger signs

The more you ride your bike, the quicker the various moving parts, particularly tires and brake pads, will wear away. Replacing the parts as soon as they become worn not only keeps the bike running smoothly but also reduces the chances of an accident. You will save money, too, since worn parts have the effect of wearing out other parts.

As you run through your safety checks (see pp.32–3), look for worn teeth on cogs and chainrings, worn brake pads, split or frayed cables, worn wheel rims, bulging or split tires, and worn tire treads. If you spot any danger signs, take action as soon as you can. You must replace a damaged part before you next ride your bike.

Checking for danger
Regularly check the tires, rims, brakes, chainrings, cables, and cogs so that you can spot signs of wear as early as possible.

Cables

Rims and tires

Brakes

Cogs

Chainrings

Cogs and chainrings
Worn teeth

Regularly check for worn or missing teeth on a chainring or cog. The chain can jump when you apply pressure to the pedals, especially if you are out of the saddle, and you may be pitched forward and crash. Replace the chainring or cog as soon as you see this sign (see pp.66–9).

Brakes
Worn brake pads

Regularly check all the brake pads for uneven wear. This is a sign that they are not contacting the braking surface evenly. The effectiveness of your brakes is compromised because not all the pad's surface is in use. Install new pads and adjust your brakes correctly (see pp.118–23).

Cables
Split or frayed cables

Check all cables and cable housings for signs of splitting and fraying. Frayed inner cables can snap, leaving you without gears, which is inconvenient, or without brakes, which is dangerous. Change the cable before you ride again (*see pp.46–9, 112–15*). Worn or split housings reduce the effectiveness of your brakes and allow dirt to get in and clog the cables. Change the housing as soon as you can.

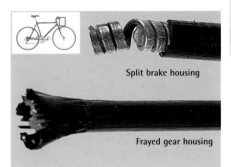

Split brake housing

Frayed gear housing

Rims and tires
Worn rim

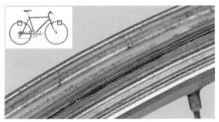

Look for evidence of deep scoring on the rims of each of your bike's wheels. Rim brakes will gradually wear out the rims, especially if you ride off-road or in winter. Eventually, the rims will fail and you could crash. Cracks around the nipples of the spokes where they join the rim are a danger sign, too. Replace the rim if you see these signs.

Bulging tire

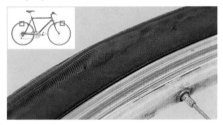

Check the whole circumference of both tires for bulges in the tread or the walls. Tires with bulges or distortions are very likely to blow out if you ride on them. If you see any of these signs, replace the tire (*see pp.104–5*).

Split tire

Check each tire for splits or cuts in the tread or side walls. A large split means that the internal fabric of the tire is damaged, so the tire is likely to blow out. Smaller splits and cuts will let sharp objects penetrate the tire, causing at least a puncture and possibly a rapid blowout. Replace the tire if you see any splits or cuts (*see pp.104–5*).

Worn tread

Look closely at the tread of both tires for signs of wear. If the tread is worn, the tire has lost structural strength and can break down and distort or bulge. The result can be a blowout during the course of a single ride. A tire that has been skidded and lost enough rubber to develop a flat spot can also be dangerous. Replace the tire if you see either sign (*see pp.104–5*).

Preparing for wet weather

These steps will help you to prepare a bike for a rainy winter, a particularly wet climate, or if most of your riding is done off-road. The mud, sand, and water that your wheels spray up into every part of the bike combine to form a damaging, grinding paste. Salt, if used to treat roads where ice is likely to occur, will quickly corrode your bike. Regular cleaning and lubricating helps with protection, but try to stop the mud and salt from reaching the delicate parts of the bike in the first place. The overall aim when protecting a bike in wet weather is to prevent water from reaching the interior parts and washing the lubricant off the exposed parts.

Protecting a bike
Fit mudguards, insert seals, and lubricate the exposed parts to protect a bike from wet conditions.

Mudguard

Headset

Derailleur

Seat post collar

Pedal

Chain

Shielding exposed components

Sealing the seat post collar

Keep water out of the point where the seat pin enters the frame. Mark this junction and remove the pin. Pull a piece of narrow road-bike inner tube over the frame. Insert the pin through the tube to the mark and tie-wrap the tube to secure it.

Sealing the headset

Place a cover over the headset to provide protection. You can fit a protector to the headset without removing any components by simply fastening the velcro.

Fitting mudguards

Fasten a mudguard to the seat pin and you will block much of the spray from the back wheel. For the front wheel, fit a guard that clips onto the frame and is secured in place with tie-wraps. Full mudguards, which attach to the fork and rear dropout, give almost full protection for on-road biking but get clogged up off-road.

Weatherproofing the drivetrain

Cleaning and lubricating the chain

Lubricate and clean your chain as often as you do in summer and after every wet ride. Apply the same light lubricant that you use in the summer and then apply a heavier oil, which will not wash off as easily. Only coat the rollers and insides of each link with heavier oil because it attracts more dirt.

Cleaning and lubricating derailleurs

Dribble oil on to the pivots around which the front and rear derailleurs move. Use a heavier, wet oil rather than the oil you would normally apply during the summer. Every time you dribble oil like this, first flush out the old oil by dribbling some degreaser onto the pivots and letting it sink in for a few minutes.

Cleaning and lubricating pedals

Apply heavier, wet oil to lubricate the retention mechanism of clipless pedals after degreasing all the moving parts. The heavier oil will not wash off as easily as dry oil. Regularly clean off old oil with degreaser and apply new oil in order to prevent the accumulation of grit and the consequent increase in pedal wear.

3

MAINTAINING YOUR

The drivetrain is the heart of your bike. Fine-tune and regularly service the system to ensure that the gear-shifters, chain, crankset, cassette, and derailleurs work together in perfect harmony.

DRIVETRAIN

CABLES AND SHIFTERS

Cables and shifters enable the rider to operate the gears. Cables are under constant tension and need to be replaced regularly and kept well lubricated. They must also be inspected often and replaced if they show signs of wear. Shifters require only occasional lubrication of their inner workings.

How they work

An inner cable connects the gear-shift lever to the derailleur, and allows the rider to change gears. Moving the gear-shift lever causes the front derailleur to shift the chain from one chainring to another, or the rear derailleur to shift the chain from one cog to another. Pulling the gear cable shifts the chain from a smaller to a larger chainring or cog; releasing the gear cable shifts the chain from a larger to a smaller chainring or cog. The left-hand shifter controls the front derailleur; the right-hand shifter controls the rear derailleur.

Controlling the gears
The cables and shifters on a bike allow the rider to effortlessly control the gear system.

Cable clamp
Attaches the cable to the rear derailleur

Rear derailleur
Moves the chain from one cog to another

REAR DERAILLEUR CABLE

A clamp connects the cable to the rear derailleur. When the shifter is pushed, the cable pulls the rear derailleur inward, moving the chain from a smaller to a larger cog. When the shifter releases the cable tension, the springs on the rear derailleur pull the jockey pulleys, and the chain, back to a smaller cog.

Front derailleur
Moves the chain from one chainring to another

SHIFTING GEAR

In this Campagnolo shifter, the rider pushes the inner shift lever to pull the cable and move the derailleur. When the rider presses a lever on the inner side of the lever hood, the cable is released and the derailleur moves back.

Gear-shift lever
Pulls and releases the gear cable

COMBINED BRAKE LEVER/GEAR-SHIFT LEVER ANATOMY

Gear-shift levers are often combined with the brake levers on the handlebar. On this Shimano shifter, the brake lever also acts as a shift lever. When the rider pushes the brake lever inward with the fingers, the control cable attached to it is pulled and a ratchet mechanism is lifted. One click of this mechanism equals one shift of the front or rear derailleur, which moves the chain across the chainring or cogs. The ratchet mechanism then holds the cable in its new position. When the rider pushes the inner shift lever inward, the ratchet mechanism's hold is released and the pull on the cable ceases.

Cable
Connects the lever to the rear derailleur

Lever hood
Attaches the levers to the handlebar

Ratchet mechanism
Holds the cable

Cable inner
Controls derailleur

Inner shift lever
Releases the cable

Cable housing
Counteracts the cable pull

Brake lever
Pulls the cable

Drop handlebar gear cables

Keeping gear cables clean and lubricated, and replacing them if they fray, is very important for smooth shifting. Change them as a matter of course at least once a year, or more often if you are a heavy user.

Lubrication reduces the effects of friction between the inner cable and the cable housing, and helps to keep out water and grit. If the gears become difficult to shift to a different chainring or cog, the cable is probably dry and needs lubrication.

These steps show how to fit a new gear cable to a SRAM shifter. Fitting cables to gear shifters made by other manufacturers, such as Shimano and Campagnolo, will be slightly different, but the order of each task in the overall sequence is generally the same.

STEP LOCATOR

Parts of gear-shift units

Rubber brake hood cover

Gear-shift lever

SRAM shifter

Brake lever

Toolbox

- Allen key multi-tool ● Long-nosed pliers
- Cable cutters ● Oil

Replacing a SRAM gear cable

1 **Use the shifter to move the chain** to the smallest sprocket if you are fitting a new rear-derailleur gear cable, or to the smallest chainring for a new front-derailleur gear cable.

- To do this with Shimano and SRAM shifters, move the inner shift lever toward the center line of the bike.

- To do this with Campagnolo shifters, push down on the lever situated on the inner side of the lever hoods.

4 **Insert the new, lubricated cable** into the same hole in the shifter that the old cable emerged from, pushing until you see it emerge from behind the lever hood.

- Pull the new cable all the way through the shifter until the nipple fits snugly in place.

2 **Undo the cable clamp bolt** on the derailleur, then release the old cable and push it through the guidance boss on the derailleur.

- Note the path by which the cable enters the derailleur and how it sits in the cable clamp. You must replicate this with the new cable.

- If the cable is frayed, cut off the frayed end with a pair of cable cutters, to allow it to pass through the guidance boss and the outer cables.

3 **Remove the old cable** from a SRAM or Campagnolo shifter by rolling the rubber lever-hood cover forward. Push the cable from behind the shifter and watch where the cable nipple emerges from the side of the shifter hood body.

- For Shimano shifters the cable emerges from under the hood cover without rolling it forward.

- Pull the old cable from the shifter by its nipple.

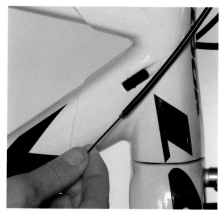

5 **Dribble a little oil into the cable outers** and insert the cable through the outers. Make sure they are firmly seated in the cable guides on the frame. If you are fitting new outers, cut them to the same length as the ones they replace.

- Ensure metal ferrules are fitted to both ends of each outer.

6 **Pull the cable through** all the outers and cable guides, and reconnect it to the derailleur by tightening the cable clamp bolt.

- Refasten the cable so that it is in exactly the same position as it was when you unfastened the clamp bolt in Step 2.

- Ensure that you pull the cable tight through the clamp bolt before you fasten it.

Straight handlebar gear cables

Looking after and replacing the gear cables on a mountain bike is very similar to a road bike. However, mountain bikes are often subjected to harsher conditions than road bikes, as they are often ridden through dirt and mud, so the cables must be replaced and lubricated more regularly.

There are three main kinds of straight handlebar shifter: the Shimano Rapidfire, the Shimano Dual Control, and the SRAM. Replacing a gear cable is similar for them all.

STEP LOCATOR

Parts of gear-shift units

SRAM shifter
Gear-shift levers
Shifter cover
Barrel adjuster
Gear indicator
Star nut
Ring clamp

Shimano Rapidfire
Gear-shift levers
Barrel adjuster

Shimano Dual Control
Gear-shift lever
Handlebar clamp
Cable port
Brake lever body
Shifter body
Brake/gear-shift lever

Toolbox
● 5mm Allen key ● Long-nosed pliers
● Cable cutters ● Cable pullers ● Tweezers

Replacing a Rapidfire gear cable

1 **Remove the old cable** with long-nosed pliers and put the shifter in the smallest sprocket or chainring position.

● Insert the end of the new, lubricated cable into the hole where the cable nipple sits inside the shifter.

● Check the route of your existing cable and follow the route when fitting a new cable in Step 4.

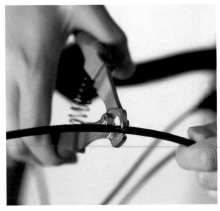

3 **Cut both the cable and cable outers** with your cable cutters to the same length as the old ones you have removed. Make the outers long enough to allow the cable to travel freely inside.

● Dribble a drop of oil down each cable outer.

● Fit a ferrule to the end of each cable outer to ensure that it fits tightly into the frame's cable guides (see pp.26–7).

Replacing a SRAM gear cable

2 **Push the cable** into the hole until its end shows through the barrel adjuster on the outside of the shifter body.

● Thread the cable through the first length of lubricated cable outer.

1 **For the rear cable,** put the shifter into the smallest sprocket. For the front cable, put the front shifter into the smallest chainring. Remove the old cable from the derailleur, then undo the star nut that holds the shifter cover in place.

● Grab the cable nipple with tweezers and remove it. Insert a new one through the barrel adjuster and seat the nipple into position. Pass the cable through the outers and reattach it to the derailleur.

Replacing a Dual Control gear cable

4 **Thread the inner cable** through each length of outer cable.

● For the rear derailleur, unscrew the barrel adjuster to about half its range and then insert the inner cable. For the front derailleur, insert the cable into the clamp.

● Pull hard with your cable pullers and tighten the cable clamp. Cut off any excess cable.

1 **For the rear cable,** put the shifter into the smallest sprocket. For the front cable, put the front shifter into the smallest chainring.

● Open the cable port to reveal the old cable inside the shifter, and remove it with long-nosed pliers.

● Push the cable into the cable port until the cable nipple sits in the cradle inside the body.

● Follow Step 4 of Replacing a Rapidfire gear cable.

FRONT AND REAR DERAILLEURS

The derailleurs move the chain smoothly between cogs and chainrings, but only if the travel of the derailleurs is set up correctly. Derailleur pivots and jockey pulleys must be checked for wear and lubricated. The front derailleur must be properly aligned with the chainrings.

How they work

The front and rear derailleurs change the gears. To change up a gear, the shifter is used to pull on the cable, which causes the front derailleur to push the chain from a smaller to a larger chainring or the rear derailleur to push the chain from a smaller to a larger cog. To change down a gear, the cable is released, causing the springs in both derailleurs to move the chain to a smaller chainring or cog. Each derailleur moves around a pivot point. Adjusting screws ensure that the derailleurs do not push the chain beyond the largest chainring or cog, or pull it beyond the smallest. This range is called the derailleur's travel. Once its travel is set up, provided the cable tension is sufficient, the derailleur will make a single, clean gear-shift for every click of the shifter.

Rear derailleur
Moves chain from one cog to another

Cable
Pushes and pulls rear derailleur

REAR DERAILLEUR ANATOMY

To change gears, two jockey pulleys transfer the chain onto a different cog. They move in the same plane as the chain and are spring-loaded to preserve the tension in the chain. Two derailleur plates enable the jockey pulleys to change gear upward, while the plate spring enables the jockey pulleys to change gear downward.

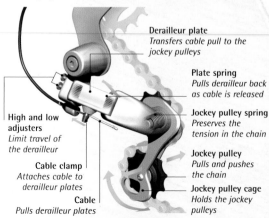

Derailleur plate
Transfers cable pull to the jockey pulleys

Plate spring
Pulls derailleur back as cable is released

High and low adjusters
Limit travel of the derailleur

Jockey pulley spring
Preserves the tension in the chain

Cable clamp
Attaches cable to derailleur plates

Jockey pulley
Pulls and pushes the chain

Cable
Pulls derailleur plates

Jockey pulley cage
Holds the jockey pulleys

Working with the shifters
The front and rear derailleurs work in harmony with the shifters to provide easy, quick, and accurate gear-shifts whenever the rider needs them.

REAR DERAILLEUR IN USE

When the cable is pulled, it causes both the derailleur plates to swing inward on four pivot points, causing the jockey pulleys to guide the chain onto a larger cog. When the cable is released, the plate spring moves the chain back to a smaller cog.

Large cog *The chain is moved to the largest cog by the pull of the cable.*

Small cog *The chain is returned to the smallest cog by the plate spring.*

FRONT DERAILLEUR ANATOMY

When pulled, the cable moves the outer arm, which acts as a lever on a pivot point to push the front derailleur cage away from the bike. This moves the chain from a smaller to a larger chainring. When the cable is released, a spring on the derailleur's inner arm pulls the cage back toward the bike.

High and low adjusters
Limits travel of the derailleur cage

Clamp bolt
Fixes derailleur to the frame

Outer arm
Acts as a lever

Cable clamp
Holds the cable to the derailleur

Pivot point
Acts as a fulcrum for the arm

Derailleur cage
Moves the chain

Chainring
Engages the chain

Front derailleur
Transfers the chain from one chainring to another

Chainring
Carries the chain

Front derailleur

Front derailleurs shift the chain from one chainring to the next. There are two main kinds: braze-on derailleurs (*below*) are fixed by an Allen bolt to a lug, or protrusion, on the bike frame; band-on derailleurs are attached to a band that goes around the frame and is part of the derailleur.

There are two important maintenance jobs for a front derailleur: setting it up after fitting a new control cable and adjusting it when it is not shifting properly. You should also clean the derailleur regularly to prevent the buildup of dirt, which interferes with the way it works and will quickly wear it out.

For the derailleur to work perfectly, the lower edge of the derailleur cage's outer side should be no higher than 2mm above the largest chainring. The cage's outer side must also be parallel with the chainrings.

Correct shifts depend on the front derailleur's traveling a certain distance per shift. High and low adjusting screws on the derailleur will control this travel.

STEP LOCATOR

Parts of a braze-on front derailleur

Cable-fixing clamp
Pivots
High/low adjusters

Front derailleur cage (outer side)
Frame-fixing clamp

Front derailleur cage (inner side)

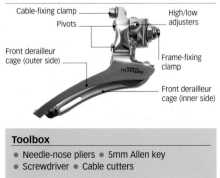

Toolbox

- Needle-nose pliers • 5mm Allen key
- Screwdriver • Cable cutters

Adjusting a front derailleur

1 **Shift the chain** onto the largest cog and the smallest chainring.

- Pull the front derailleur cage away from the frame. The lower edge of its outer side should clear the largest chainring by 2mm. If it is more or less, undo the frame-fixing clamp and raise or lower the front derailleur.

- Line up the cage parallel with the chainrings and tighten the frame-fixing clamp.

3 **Pull the gear cable** through the cable clamp and tighten the cable-clamp bolt.

- Cut off any excess cable with your cable cutters and put on a cable crimp (*see pp.26–7*).

- Repeat Steps 2 and 3 if, after a couple of rides, the chain will not shift up to the next chainring, since cables can sometimes stretch slightly.

2 **Undo the cable-fixing clamp** until the cable comes free.

● Look for the low gear adjuster (usually marked "L") and screw it in or out until the inner side of the front derailleur cage is about 2mm from the chain. You have now set the starting point of the derailleur's travel.

● Take this opportunity to clean the guide in which the cable runs under the bottom-bracket shell. Use degreaser, and then wash and dry the whole area.

● Put a little dry lubricant in the guide.

4 **Shift the chain** across until it is on the smallest cog and the largest chainring.

● Repeat Steps 2 and 3 if the chain will not shift onto the largest chainring.

5 **Screw in the high adjuster** (usually marked "H") to bring the outer side of the front derailleur cage to about 2mm from the chain.

● Unscrew the higher adjuster to allow more travel if, when you shift to the largest chainring, the chain does not move onto it.

● Check the action by shifting a few times between all the chainrings.

Rear derailleur

Most rear derailleurs are indexed, which means that for every click of the shifter, either up or down, the derailleur will shift the chain from one cog to the next.

Occasionally, you may find that the chain does not quite move onto the next cog when you make a single shift, or else it skips a cog in an overshift. In either case, the rear derailleur needs adjusting. You will also need to follow the steps in this sequence whenever you fit a new cable (see pp.46–9).

To ensure that the rear derailleur works faultlessly, pay particular attention to its jockey pulleys because this is where oil and dirt can accumulate. Degrease and scrub them every time you clean your bike (see pp.28–9). Whenever you lubricate the jockey pulleys or the rear derailleur pivots, make sure you wipe off any excess oil.

STEP LOCATOR

Parts of a rear derailleur

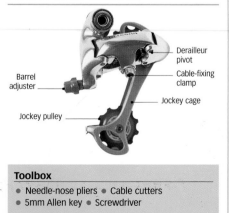

Derailleur pivot
Cable-fixing clamp
Jockey cage
Barrel adjuster
Jockey pulley

Toolbox

- Needle-nose pliers ● Cable cutters
- 5mm Allen key ● Screwdriver

Adjusting a rear derailleur

1 **Shift the chain** onto the biggest chainring and smallest cog, then undo the cable-fixing clamp so that the cable hangs free.

● Check the cable and fit a new one if it shows any sign of fraying (see p.39).

● Screw the barrel adjuster in or out, until it is at half of its range.

4 **Shift back to the smallest cog,** then shift upward through each gear. If the rear derailleur does not shift all the way onto the next-biggest cog, screw out the barrel adjuster until it does. If the derailleur overshifts and skips a cog, screw in the barrel adjuster until it stops.

2 **Use the high adjuster** (usually marked "H") to line up the jockey pulleys with the smallest cog.

● Once you have lined them up, rotate the pedals forward while adjusting the "H" adjuster until the chain runs smoothly.

● Pull the cable downward through the cable-fixing clamp and reclamp it.

3 **Shift onto the smallest chainring** and largest cog.

● Push the rear derailleur with your fingers toward the spokes. If it moves beyond the largest cog, screw in the low adjuster (marked "L") until the derailleur stops at the largest cog.

● Turn the pedals to see if the chain runs smoothly. If it does not, adjust the "L" in or out.

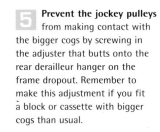

5 **Prevent the jockey pulleys** from making contact with the bigger cogs by screwing in the adjuster that butts onto the rear derailleur hanger on the frame dropout. Remember to make this adjustment if you fit a block or cassette with bigger cogs than usual.

HUB GEARS

Hub gears located inside the hub casing alter the speed at which the back wheel revolves. They require little routine maintenance and, since they are sealed, most hub-gear systems do not need to be lubricated regularly. The control cables must still be inspected regularly and replaced if they are worn.

How they work

All hub gears work according to the same basic principle. A system of internal cogs makes the hub casing, and therefore the rear wheel, turn at a different speed from a single, external cog that is driven by the pedals via the chain. The external cog is connected to the internal cogs by a driver unit, and the cogs rotate the hub casing at different speeds. Spokes attach the casing to the rim, thereby turning the rear wheel.

A shifter on the handlebar operates a mechanism attached to the hub. This mechanism causes various combinations of different-sized cogs within the hub to engage with a ring gear, which drives the hub casing. Each combination gives a different gear ratio, and the number of gears depends on the number of cogs within the hub.

SHIMANO NEXUS HUB GEAR ANATOMY

To change gear, the rider activates the shifter to pull the cable, which turns the satellite on the drive side of the hub. This triggers a mechanism within the driver unit to move two carrier units containing cogs. Different cogs are brought into contact with the ring gears. When the cable is released, the spring-loaded carrier units move the cogs back to a different combination.

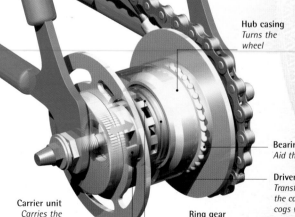

Hub casing
Turns the wheel

Cable and satellite
Side view of the hub

Bearings
Aid the rotation of the hub casing

Driver unit
Transfers the cog's drive and causes the carrier unit to engage different cogs with the ring gear

Carrier unit
Carries the different-sized cogs

Ring gear
Turns the hub casing

Protecting the gears
The hub gear mechanism is fully enclosed to protect it from damage, dirt, and water.

Hub gear unit
Contains the cogs that allow gear changes

Hub gear I

If the cable to your hub gear breaks or frays, you will need to replace it. Before you start, first identify the hub gear units on your bike from the manufacturer's name. This is usually stamped on the hub, and the number of gears is indicated on the shifter.

The hub-gear model illustrated in the steps of this sequence is the Shimano Nexus 7-speed gear, which is operated by a twist-grip shifter. Alternatively, bikes may be equipped with SRAM hub gears, as well as those made by other manufacturers, that are operated by thumbshifters.

Some older bikes have Sturmey Archer 3-speed gears. Although they all work on the same principle, the methods used to change a cable are subtly different. Try to find the manufacturer's instructions for the gear on your bike—ask at a bike shop or search the Internet.

STEP LOCATOR

Parts of a hub gear

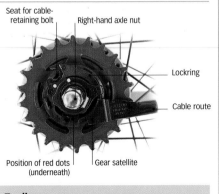

Seat for cable-retaining bolt

Right-hand axle nut

Lockring

Cable route

Position of red dots (underneath)

Gear satellite

Toolbox

- Wrenches to fit wheel axle nuts and cable-clamp bolt • Flat-bladed screwdriver

Replacing a hub-gear cable

1 **Put the shifter into first gear.** At this point, there is no tension on the cable, so it is the starting point for fitting a new cable. If the cable is broken, the hub gear will have automatically returned to first gear, so move the shifter there to line up the system.

4 **Insert the cable** through the chainstay cable guide and make sure the housing is well-seated into the guide.

- Pull the cable tight and tighten the clamp bolt onto it at exactly the distance you measured from the cable guide in Step 2.

- Now push the clamp bolt back into the place where it sits on the gear satellite (*inset*).

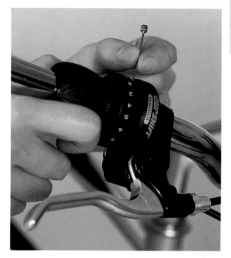

2 **Remove the rear wheel** and push the wheel forward out of the dropout.

- Use a flat screwdriver to lever out the cable-clamp bolt from the position in which it sits on the gear satellite.

- Pull on the clamp bolt and measure the length of the cable between it and the chainstay cable guide. Undo the clamp to remove it from the old cable.

3 **Remove the cable port** on the plastic part of the shifter, where the pointer indicates which gear the system is in.

- Take the old cable out of the shifter by pushing it from behind, or pull it out by its nipple.

- Insert the greased new cable into the shifter. Dribble a little oil inside the housing and then push the new cable through the housing.

5 **Return the wheel to the bike** by placing the axle in the rear dropouts and pulling backward on the wheel so that there is tension on the chain. Do not pull so hard that the chain becomes tight.

- Ensure that the wheel is straight between the chainstays and tighten the axle nuts. There should be about ¼in (6mm) of vertical play in the chain.

- Run through the gears, shift by shift. If there is a problem, the hub gear may need adjusting (*see pp.60–1*).

Hub gear II

Occasionally, you might be unable to engage a particular gear because dirt has interfered with the gear satellite's action. You will need to remove the satellite to clean it, and this means removing the rear wheel.

On other occasions, you might find that the shift has lost some of its smoothness. In this case, the cable has probably stretched so that the shifter is out of phase with the gear mechanism. To remedy this problem, use the barrel adjuster on the shifter to take up any slack in the cable.

Every time the wheel is removed and put back on to your bike, run through the gears and make sure they are shifting correctly. If they are not, follow the last two steps of this sequence in order to make the gears run smoothly.

Finally, the hub-gear system has clear markings—look for the red dots and the yellow dots and triangles—to help you to set up the gears.

If a bike is fitted with a Sturmey Archer 3-speed hub gear, it may occasionally shift to second gear, but without any drive. When this happens, put the shifter into the third-gear position and look at the cable where it runs along the chainstay. The cable will be slack so that it sags. Undo the cable-clamp bolt near the hub-gear unit and pull the cable through the clamp until it runs in a straight line. Reclamp the bolt and the gears will shift perfectly.

Adjusting your hub-gear assembly

1 **Remove the rear wheel** by undoing and removing both its axle bolts. The satellite is locked onto the hub by a lockring. Turn the lockring by hand until its yellow dot lines up with the one on the satellite.

● Lift off the lockring to free the satellite.

3 **Put the satellite back** onto the wheel. Line up its triangles with those on the axle.

● Press the satellite home on to the hub.

● Replace the lockring, pushing it onto the satellite so that its yellow dot lines up with the yellow dot on the satellite.

● Turn the lockring so that the dots are separated. The satellite is now locked in place.

STEP LOCATOR

Toolbox

● Wrenches to fit wheel axle nuts

2 **Lift the satellite** from the hub body, noting the relative positions of the two yellow triangles that are marked on it.

● Note the position of two more yellow triangles on the bare axle that is left inside the wheel.

● Flush out the freed gear satellite with degreaser. Let this drain out and spray light oil into the satellite.

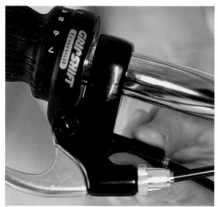

4 **Shift through the gears** until the shifter is in fourth gear.

● Use the barrel adjuster on the shifter to fine-tune the gear adjustment. Tilt the bike so that you can see the underside of the hub gear.

5 **Look for the two red dots** on the gear mechanism. One is marked on the satellite and one on the lockring. Both dots are marked on the underside of the gear where the cable runs. In fourth gear, these two dots should line up. If they do not, screw the barrel adjuster in or out until the dots line up. When they do line up, all the gear-shifts will be perfect.

CHAIN, CASSETTE, AND CRANKSET

With every turn of the pedals, the chain, cassette, and crankset are put under strain. The parts are in continual contact, and the motion of pedaling inevitably leads to wear. No matter how well you care for each part, they eventually need to be removed and replaced.

How they work

The chain, cassette, and crankset combine to form the heart of the drivetrain, the part of the bike through which a rider's pedal power is transferred into forward motion. The pedals drive the crankset and, via the chain, turn a cog attached to the hub of the rear wheel, which in turn rotates the wheel.

Bikes with derailleur gears use derailleurs to shift the chain onto different-sized cogs and chainrings, which make up the cassette and crankset. Each combination of chainring and cog provides a different gear ratio, giving up to 27 different gears that can be used to tackle anything from steep climbs to gentle flats.

Chain
Feeds through jockey pulleys

Rear derailleur
Shifts the chain across the cogs

Cogs
Driven by the chain

EXPLODED CASSETTE

The cassette transfers the motion of the chain to the wheel. It consists of cogs that slide onto the cassette body, which is bolted onto the hub. The cassette body houses the freewheel, which allows the wheel to turn when the cassette is stationary.

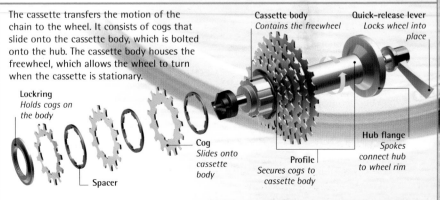

Cassette body
Contains the freewheel

Quick-release lever
Locks wheel into place

Lockring
Holds cogs on the body

Cog
Slides onto cassette body

Profile
Secures cogs to cassette body

Hub flange
Spokes connect hub to wheel rim

Spacer

CHAIN ANATOMY

The chain is the key to transmitting pedal power into forward motion.

To transfer power efficiently, the chain must be strong, but flexible enough to fit securely around the teeth of the chainrings and cogs. To achieve this, a series of links articulate around joining pins, which are surrounded by revolving metal barrels.

Joining pin
Connects inner and outer links

Barrel
Sits between teeth of chainrings and cogs

Outer link
Shaped to allow quick gear-shifts

Inner link
Rotates around the barrel

Rear wheel
Driven by the cogs

Crankset
Powered by pedaling

Chainring
Carries the chain around the crankset

Chain
Transmits power from the crankset

Pedal
Transmits energy to the crankset

Lightweight components
The chain, cassette, and crankset are lightweight items that use the latest design and construction techniques to maximize strength and durability while maintaining an aerodynamic profile.

Chains

Replacing a chain is a regular maintenance task. All chains eventually wear out, even if you clean and lubricate them properly. A worn chain, as well as being inefficient, will quickly wear out other drive parts and end up costing you money.

To determine how much a chain has worn, either use a specialist gauge from a bike shop or measure the length of 24 links. If the length is greater than 12in (300mm), the chain is worn.

New chains on derailleur gear systems are linked with a joining pin that comes with the chain. You will need a link extractor tool to make this join. The thicker chains of hub gears, BMX bikes, and some fixed-gear bikes are joined by split links.

STEP LOCATOR

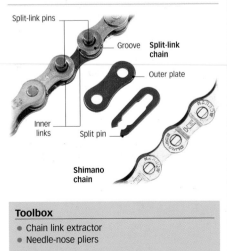

Parts of a split-link and a Shimano chain

Split-link pins

Groove **Split-link chain**

Outer plate

Inner links

Split pin

Shimano chain

Toolbox

- Chain link extractor
- Needle-nose pliers

Replacing a derailleur chain

1 **Shift onto the smallest chainring** and cog so that the chain is slack.

- Place a link in the link extractor and push out the pin until the chain breaks.
- Remove the old chain with the link extractor.

3 **Remove the excess links** from the opposite end from the one on which there is a joining link. Leave an inner link so that the two ends can be joined together.

- Close the chain by pushing the pin of the joining link through the opposite inner link with the extractor tool.

Joining a split-link chain

2 **Thread a new chain** through the jockey pulleys and around the biggest chainring and smallest cog.

- Pull the ends of the chain together so that there is a little tension in the jockey pulleys. This establishes the length of chain you need.

1 **Join the chain** by pressing the side of the split link with the pins fixed in its plate through the two inner-link ends of the chain.

- Press the other plate onto the pins that are now sticking through the inner links.

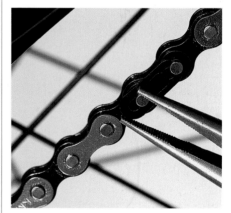

4 **Loosen any stiff links** that occur when the chain links are compressed during Step 3.

- Flex the stiff links with a little sideways pressure until they become loose (*inset*).

- Remove the protruding part of the pin after joining a Shimano chain, since these have an extra-long joining pin.

- Break off the excess with needle-nose pliers.

2 **Push the split pin** into the grooves of the split-link pins. These are sticking through the outer plate that you have just fitted. The split pin's open end should face the rear of the bike.

- Fix the split pin in place by pushing it home with needle-nose pliers until you feel it click.

Cassette and freewheel

The cassette and freewheel allow the rear wheel to rotate while the pedals remain stationary. Their internal mechanisms—the freehub body of a cassette and the block in a freewheel—will eventually wear out and need replacing. The cogs on both can also wear down. These parts will also need to be removed whenever you replace a broken spoke on the drive side of the rear wheel.

The tools for removing a freewheel and a cassette depend on the manufacturer of the part that is fitted to the bike. Usually, the manufacturer's name is stamped on the component. However, if you are in any doubt about which tool you need, take the wheel to the bike shop when buying a remover tool.

STEP LOCATOR

Parts of a freewheel and a cassette

Cog

Freewheel mechanism

Cogs

Inner side ridges of cassette

Freewheel

Lockring

Cassette

Toolbox

- Wrenches ● Cassette remover ● Chain whip
- Block remover ● Grease

Removing a cassette

1 **Remove the quick-release skewer** from the rear wheel.

● Insert the cassette remover into the teeth of the lockring at the center of the cassette.

● Replace the quick-release skewer to secure the cassette remover.

Removing a freewheel block

1 **Remove the quick-release skewer** and insert the block remover into the teeth at the block's center.

● Lock the block remover in place by replacing the quick-release skewer.

2 **Wrap the chain whip** around a cog, and place the wrench on the remover.

● Press downward on both tools. This holds the cassette, while the remover unlocks the lockring.

● Remove the quick-release skewer once the lockring starts turning.

● Continue to unscrew the lockring with the cassette remover.

3 **Take off the smallest cog** after you have removed the lockring. On many cassettes, the remaining cogs come off in one piece. If they do not, you must put individual cogs back in a certain way. Failure to do so will affect the precision of gear-shifts. Usually, the cogs are marked, so that lining up these marks ensures the correct cog orientation.

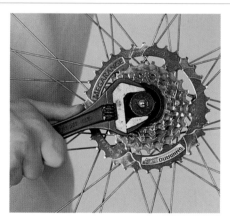

2 **Put the wrench** on the flats of the block remover and turn counterclockwise.

● As the block begins to move, remove the quick-release skewer and continue turning until the block comes off.

3 **Check the integral freewheel mechanism,** which is independent of the hub. Replace it with a new block if it is worn.

● Coat the threads of the hub with grease, then screw the block on by hand.

● Lock the block in place by tightening it with the wrench and the block remover.

Cranksets

Removing a crankset is a useful skill to have because it will allow you to replace an old crankarm, clean or replace a worn chainring, or work on the bottom bracket.

Cranksets are attached in one of four ways. Those held in place by a hexagonal bolt can be removed with a crankset socket spanner (see *Step 1*). Cranksets with a self-removing Allen bolt can be detached with an 8mm Allen key (see *Step 2*). Versions with a standard Allen bolt can be detached with the relevant Allen key (see *Step 3*). Those on a hollow-axle bottom bracket can be removed by reversing the steps on pp.74–5.

When refitting a crankset, keep grease or oil from touching the axle. The crankset must be dry when fitted to the axle or it will work loose. After refitting, go for a short ride and then try the axle bolt again. If it is slightly loose, you should tighten it.

STEP LOCATOR

Parts of a crankset

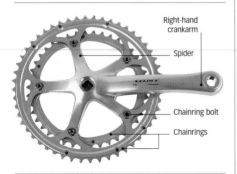

Right-hand crankarm

Spider

Chainring bolt

Chainrings

Toolbox

- Crank extractor ● 5mm Allen key
- 8mm Allen key or crankset socket spanner
- Chainring bolt peg spanner

Removing a crankset

1 **Detach a hexagonal crankset bolt** from the axle with a crankset socket wrench. Normal socket wrenches are often too thick to fit into the space where the bolt is located.

- Steady the crankarm with your free hand to give you something to push against. Work from below the crankset so that if your hand slips, the chainring teeth will not injure you.

- To remove the crankset, go to Step 4.

4 **Use a crank extractor** to remove the crankset if it is not the self-removing type. Make sure that the washer beneath the bolt has also been removed.

- Carefully screw the extractor into the delicate threads at the centre of the crankset. When the extractor is fully in, turn its handle clockwise to pull off the crankset.

2 **Unscrew a self-removing Allen bolt** with an 8mm Allen key. These bolts extract the crankset as you unscrew them.

● Steady the crankarm with your free hand to give you something to push against. Work from below the crankset so that if your hand slips, the chainring teeth will not injure you.

● To remove the chainring, go to Step 5.

3 **Use a long-handled Allen key** if there is an Allen bolt holding the crankset on your bike. Usually, an 8mm key is the size required.

● Work from below the crankset so that if you slip, the chainring teeth will not injure you.

● To remove the crankset, go to Step 4.

5 **Remove the chainring** with a 5mm Allen key on one side and a chainring bolt peg spanner to hold the bolt on the other. You can do this without taking the crankset off the axle, but you must remove it if you are working on the inner rings of some triple cranksets.

● Cure a creaking noise from the crankset by putting grease on the threads of the chainring bolts before you reassemble the crankset. Standard chainring bolts are made from steel. Be especially careful not to over-tighten aluminium or titanium bolts.

BOTTOM BRACKETS

There are two main types of bottom bracket: cartridge-bearing and hollow-axle. Both use sealed bearings, which can wear out over time. If this happens on the cartridge version, replace the whole unit, but on a hollow-axle type you only need to replace the bearings.

How they work

The bottom bracket joins the crank of each pedal with an axle, which rotates in the bike's frame. Each type of bracket consists of an axle, two bearings, and two threaded cups (called either the free cup and fixed cup, or the non-drive and drive-side cup). With the cartridge type, both cranks bolt onto the axle, but with the hollow-axle type, the drive-side crank is fixed to the axle and only the non-drive side crank can be bolted on. A third type of bottom bracket, the BMX bracket, has a threaded axle—the bracket is held in place by a locknut that screws on to the thread on the non-drive side of the axle.

Providing strength
The axle and bearings of the bottom bracket need to be both strong and reliable enough to bear the weight and power of the rider.

CARTRIDGE-BEARING BOTTOM BRACKET ANATOMY

Each of the cartridge bearings is composed of ball bearings, which are sandwiched between an inner and outer race by plastic seals. The cartridge bearings are located close to each end of the bottom-bracket axle. A tubular sleeve fits over the two bearings, filling the space between them. The fixed and free cups fit over this sleeve to create a totally sealed unit.

Fixed cup
Holds the bottom bracket in place

Outer race
Houses the bearings

Ball-bearing
Supports the axle

Axle
Connects the cranks and rotates in the bearings

Free cup
Screws into the bike's frame

Crank
Turns the axle

HOLLOW-AXLE BOTTOM BRACKET ANATOMY

The drive-side crank is permanently fixed to the axle, which passes through both cups. The non-drive side crank slides onto the axle and is secured by two pinch bolts. The crank cap bolt inserts into the end of the axle to hold the crank against the bearing, ensuring that there is no play, rather like the stem cap bolt on a threadless headset (*p.90*).

Pinch bolts
Hold crank in place on the axle

Crank cap bolt
Presses crank against bearings

Ball-bearing
Lets the axle turn

Cup
Holds bearings in the frame

Cup
Holds the bearings in place in the frame

Axle
Connects the cranks and rotates in the bearings

Crank
Turns the axle

Crank
Turns the axle

Cartridge-bearing bottom bracket
Allows the smooth rotation of the axle

Cartridge bottom bracket

Cartridge bottom brackets require no routine maintenance. Their bearings are sealed from the elements—even from the water you use for hosing or pressure-washing your bike, provided you turn the pedals forward during the wash.

When the bearings do eventually wear out, you will have to replace the whole unit. The remover tools for this job are specific to each particular bottom bracket, so check which brand is fitted to your bike before buying the tools.

If you are planning a replacement, there are three types of bottom bracket axles to choose from: square-tapered, Shimano Octalink, and Isis. The type used in the steps in this sequence is square-tapered; the type shown below is Octalink. Finally, if your bike is fitted with an Italian-threaded bottom bracket, marked 36 x 1, ask a bike shop to help with replacing it.

STEP LOCATOR

Parts of a cartridge bottom bracket

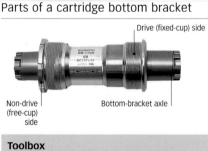

Drive (fixed-cup) side

Non-drive (free-cup) side

Bottom-bracket axle

Toolbox
- Measuring calipers • Ruler • Wrench
- Cartridge bottom bracket remover • Grease

Installing a cartridge bottom bracket

1 **Put the bike on a workstand** and remove the crankset (*see pp.68–9*).

- Use a pair of calipers to measure the length of the old axle before you remove the bottom bracket, so that you can be sure the replacement has an axle of the same length. You need to do this because different cranksets are designed to work with different axle lengths.

4 **Grease the threads** of each side of the new bottom bracket for easier fitting. The non-drive threads are sometimes referred to as the free-cup and the drive-side threads are known as the fixed cup. Do not grease the drive side of a bottom bracket with Italian threads.

2 **Measure the width** of the bottom-bracket shell with a ruler. The shell forms part of the bike's frame and will be either 2¾in (68mm) or 3in (73mm) wide. This width determines the width of the bracket unit you need to buy.

3 **Remove both the crankarms** (see pp.68–9), insert a bottom-bracket remover into the non-drive side of the bracket, and turn the remover counterclockwise with a wrench.

● Repeat on the other side, turning clockwise. Turn counterclockwise if your bike has an Italian-threaded bottom bracket (marked 36 x 1).

5 **Insert the bottom bracket** from the drive (fixed-cup) side using the remover tool. Fit the teeth of the tool into the indentations of the bottom bracket (see enlargement).

● Insert the non-drive (free-cup) side when the drive side is almost in position. Use the remover to screw it in a few turns. Fully tighten the drive side, then the non-drive side.

Hollow-axle bottom bracket

Hollow-axle bottom brackets, such as those made by SRAM, Campagnolo, and Shimano, are designed to increase bottom-bracket strength. The axle bearings screw onto the outside of the bottom bracket shell, which houses a large diameter axle that is hollow, light, and stronger than other axles. Since the bearings are farther apart than on other bottom-bracket designs, they encounter less torque, which increases their lifespan. But they will eventually wear out, so you will need to know how to remove and replace them. The steps can also be followed if you want to upgrade to this system.

STEP LOCATOR

Parts of a hollow-axle bottom bracket

Chainring

Axle

Combined drive-side cup and sleeve

Spacers

Left-hand crank

Non-drive side cup

Pinch bolt

Crank cap bolt

Toolbox

- Hollow-axle cup tool ● Hollow-axle crank cap tool
- Allen key multi-tool

Installing a hollow-axle bottom bracket

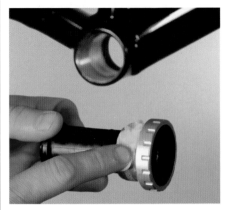

1 **The faces of the bottom** bracket shell must be flat and parallel. This requires specialist equipment, so get the frame checked at a bike shop.

- Measure the width of the bottom bracket shell, then check the manufacturer's instructions to determine how many spacers are required and on which cup to put them.

- Grease the threads of the cups and place the necessary spacers on them.

4 **Push the left-hand crank** onto the non-drive side of the axle.

- The crank must be mounted at 180-degrees to the right-hand crank. To do this, match the wide notch on the axle with the wide tooth on the crank.

- Unlike other bottom bracket systems, it is not necessary to have a dry interface between the crank and axle. Put a little grease on the axle before you fit the crank.

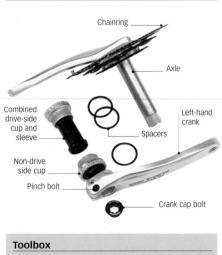

2 **Screw the cups into** the frame as far as you can with your fingers (*inset*).

● The drive-side cup screws in anti-clockwise, and the non-drive-side cup screws in clockwise.

● Secure the cups on each side by tightening them with the hollow-axle cup tool (*main image*).

● Grease the axle in preparation for pushing it through the cups.

3 **Hold the drive side** (right-hand) crank and push the axle through the hole in the center of the drive-side cup.

● Continue pushing until the end of the axle pops out of the non-drive-side cup.

● You may encounter resistance, especially as you push the axle through the non-drive side cup. If this happens, give the center of the crank a sharp tap with a plastic mallet.

5 **Grease the threads** of the crank cap bolt, and screw it into place with your fingers.

● Tighten the crank cap bolt with the crank cap tool, which draws the crank onto the axle.

● Do not over-tighten the crank cap bolt. Rotate the cranks and if the axle is stiff, loosen the crank cap bolt a little.

6 **Tighten the crank pinch** bolts with an Allen key to fix the crank in place.

● The pinch bolts work as a pair, so must be equally tight. Tighten them in sequence by screwing in the first a little, then screwing in the other by the same amount. Repeat until both bolts are tight, but do not use excessive force.

● If you have access to a torque wrench, use it to tighten the bolts to the manufacturer's instructions.

BMX bottom bracket

Many types of bottom brackets are fitted to BMX bikes. The type used in this sequence of steps is similar to the type used on many children's bikes.

The biggest difference between this kind of BMX bracket and normal bottom brackets is that the threads securing it in the frame are on the axle and not inside the bottom-bracket shell. The axle has a cup and cone bearing system, a little like an open-bearing hub (see pp.100–1). The drive-side cone, chainring, and axle are made in one piece, and the crankarms bolt on to them. This kind of crankset and bottom bracket is called a 3-piece crankset. Screwing the locknut onto the cone needs practice to ensure that the bottom bracket is adjusted successfully.

STEP LOCATOR

1 2 3 4 5 6

Parts of a BMX bottom bracket

Chainring
Drive-side cone
Non-drive side cup
Non-drive side bearings
Non-drive side cone
Drive-side bearings
Axle
Axle threads
Spacing washer
Drive-side cup
Locknut

Toolbox

- Allen key multi-tool ● Peg wrench
- Wrenches ● Grease ● Degreaser

Setting up a BMX bottom bracket

1 **Take out the captive bolt** at the center of the non-drive side crankarm, then loosen the crankarm bolt on the side.

4 **Put the newly greased** drive-side bearings back into their cup, then insert the axle so that it sticks out of the non-drive side.

● Put the greased, non-drive side bearings over the axle and into their cup.

● Make sure that the non-drive bearings are sitting square inside their cup.

Remove the crankarm. Hold the non-drive cone still with a peg wrench while removing the locknut with a wrench.

● Remove the spacer and the cone and pull out the non-drive bearings from the cup, which is located inside the bottom-bracket shell.

● Inspect, clean, and degrease the cone.

Take out the drive side of the bottom bracket once you have removed the locknut and cone from the non-drive side.

● Hold the drive side by the drive-side crankarm and clean and degrease the bearings. Replace any worn bearings and grease the clean bearings.

● Inspect the cups while the drive side is out of the bike. Replace any worn cups or cones.

Put the non-drive cone and spacer over the axle and screw the cone on to the bearings with the peg wrench. Screw the locknut onto the axle.

● Hold the cone in place against the bearings and screw the locknut down onto it. Then screw the cone back a little to the locknut. A bit of play in the axle is permissible, but too much will throw off the chain.

Put the spacer back on the non-drive side of the axle and then push the crankarm back onto it.

● Tighten the captive bolt in the middle of the crankarm, then tighten the retaining bolt on its side.

PEDALS

There are two types of pedals, flat and clipless. Pedals with open bearings require regular inspection and lubrication. Clipless pedals must be lubricated to ensure easy foot release. Cleats should be correctly fitted to the rider's shoes and regularly inspected for wear.

How they work

The two pedals transfer the push from the rider's legs and feet into both crankarms, which, in turn, rotate the axle in the bottom bracket. The body of a pedal rotates around an axle and is supported on bearings that are either open or held within a cartridge. The pedal's axle screws into the crankarm.

Pedals should grip a rider's feet in some way. For example, studs that prevent foot slippage will help a rider who makes frequent stops, such as a commuter in heavy traffic. Some flat pedals are fitted with toe-clips and straps that hold the front of the foot, although they can interfere with the foot as the rider tries to remove it. Clipless pedals hold the foot securely, while releasing it easily whenever the rider wishes.

Converting energy
Pedals are the invention that defines cycling. They are the first step in the process of converting human energy into mechanical motion.

FLAT PEDAL ANATOMY

Two bearings on the pedal's axle are held in place by a cone and lockring that screw on to the outer end of the axle. A knurled retainer attaches the pedal body to the axle. The cone (not visible) and the lockring can be adjusted to permit the free rotation of the body around the axle, without any play.

Crankarm
Transfers power to the bottom bracket

Pedal body
Rotates on the axle

Locknut
Holds the cone in place

Axle
Screws into the crankarm

Knurled retainer
Holds the body onto the axle

Ball bearings
Allow the body to rotate around the axle

Pedal
*Connects the rider's foot
to the drivetrain*

Pedal axle

The axle of a pedal is usually made from steel and the crankarms from aluminum alloy. This creates an interface where a chemical reaction can take place between the two metals, so it is important that you coat the threads with grease before you put pedals on your bike. The tools for removing the axles are specific to the brand and model of the pedals, and are either supplied with the pedals or available at a good bike shop.

Most pedals contain two bearings on which the pedal body revolves around its axle. These sometimes need replacing; in the case of ball bearings, they need regular cleaning, checking, and greasing.

Pedal axles can be damaged by an impact or during a fall, and a bent axle can cause riding discomfort or even injury. After removing the pedals, rotate their axles by hand, feeling for the tight spots that are evidence of a bent axle.

STEP LOCATOR

1 2 3 4 5 6

Parts of a pedal

Cleat-release mechanism

Pedal body

Pedal axle

Retainer

Wrench flats

Release tension adjuster

Toolbox

- 15mm bike spanner • Allen key multi-tool
- Remover tool • Degreaser • Grease

Removing and lubricating a pedal axle

1 **Place a wrench** on the flats of the axle to remove a pedal.

- Turn the wrench counterclockwise for the right pedal, which has a right-hand thread, and clockwise for the left pedal, which has a left-hand thread.

- Steady the opposite crankarm with your hand to give you something to push against.

4 **Lift the axle from the pedal** once you have fully unscrewed the retainer nut.

- Clean the axle with degreaser and inspect it. If the axle is bent, it will need to be replaced.

- Replace the bearings on the end of the axle if they are worn.

 Hold the removed pedal, with the axle upward, in a vise.

● Remove the axle by using a remover tool that fits over the knurled retainer connecting the axle to the pedal.

Ensure that the remover tool fits snugly onto the retainer. The retainer may be damaged if you do not.

● Place a wrench on the flats of the remover tool in place and turn it to remove the retainer.

● Turn the wrench clockwise for the right axle retainer, which has a left-hand thread, and counterclockwise for the left axle retainer, which has a right-hand thread.

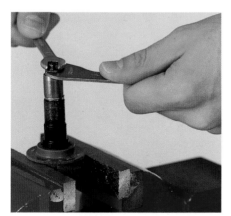

Hold the cone with one wrench and remove the locknut with another. The cone and locknut hold the bearings on the end of the axle.

● Remove the cone, then the old bearings. Clean the end of the axle.

● Set the new bearings in grease and screw the cone back on top of them. Then lock the cone with the locknut.

Grease the inner bearing to prolong its life. If it is worn, the whole axle assembly must be replaced.

● Push some grease down into the bearing after cleaning the axle. To reassemble the pedal, carry out Steps 1–4 in reverse order.

Clipless pedals

Clipless pedals were developed in response to the racing cyclist's need to apply power throughout the entire pedal revolution. They hold the foot to the pedal by locking onto a cleat attached to the sole of the shoe. The mechanism that holds the cleat is spring-loaded—the foot is released by turning the heel outward.

The release spring is an essential working part and must be kept clean and well lubricated. Use light oils on road pedals and heavier oils on off-road pedals. Wipe oil off the pedal body to stop your foot from slipping. The mechanism lets the foot pivot around its long axis during each revolution. The oil applied to the release spring is enough to keep the mechanism working well.

Toolbox
- 15mm bike wrench ● Allen key multi-tool
- Degreaser ● Stiff brush ● Oil

ROAD PEDALS

Road pedals are light, supportive, and, because of the greater speeds involved in road riding, aerodynamic. They need to engage and release the feet with equal ease, as well as holding the foot securely. Ideally, you should be able to adjust them according to how much movement your feet make during pedaling.

Time road pedal
These pedals offer a range of movement that can be adjusted to suit the requirements of individual riders. Keep them well maintained by scrubbing regularly with degreaser, using a stiff brush. Wash this off, then lubricate the release spring with heavier oil, dribbling it from a can.

Top face

Bottom face

Pedal body

Retention mechanism

Release spring

Release-tension adjuster

Look road pedal
These easy-to-maintain pedals have a small Allen bolt on top of the back plate retention mechanism, which adjusts the foot-release tension. The pedals need to be scrubbed clean regularly. Occasionally, dribble some oil between the back plate and pedal body.

Top face

Pedal body

Bottom face

Release tension adjuster

Release spring

Back plate

OFF-ROAD PEDALS

Off-road pedals are equipped with retention mechanisms on at least two sides so that the rider's feet can attach to the pedal no matter which way up it is. The pedals also let mud pass through to prevent them from becoming clogged.

Time off-road pedal
The few moving parts of this simple pedal are protected in the body of the pedal. Keep the parts clean and dribble a little heavy oil into the point where the release bar enters the pedal body. If necessary, replace the bearings and axles (see pp.80–1).

Shimano off-road pedal
The open design of this pedal allows good mud clearance but exposes the pedal's retention mechanism to the elements. Clean and degrease the pedals regularly and lubricate the moving parts with a heavy lubricant. The release tension adjuster is on the back plate of this double-sided pedal.

Crank Brothers pedal
This is an open design with excellent mud clearance and very few moving parts—the retention mechanism is just a simple spring. Clean the pedals regularly, and very occasionally re-grease the bearings using a grease gun and a special adaptor that is sold with the pedals.

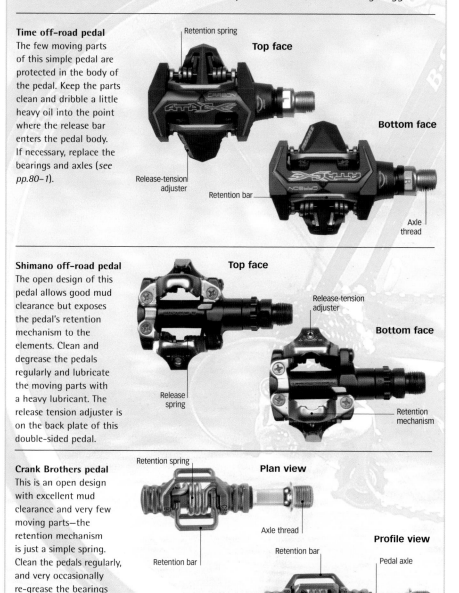

Pedal cleats

Clipless pedals are designed to hold your feet firmly in place, so it is important that the cleats on the pedals are positioned correctly on the sole of your shoes. The right position also enables you to transfer the maximum amount of leg power into the pedals.

Once you have set up the cleats, you might find that your feet try to return to their natural position as you ride. Alter the cleat's angle to accommodate this. However, do not alter its fore and aft position because the position shown here is the most efficient for applying power to the pedals.

The steps in this sequence show an off-road pedal (*see pp.82–3*), but the principles are the same for road pedals.

STEP LOCATOR

Parts of a pedal cleat

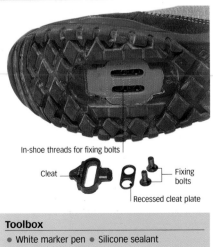

In-shoe threads for fixing bolts

Cleat

Fixing bolts

Recessed cleat plate

Toolbox

● White marker pen ● Silicone sealant
● Allen keys ● Screwdriver

Fitting a pedal cleat

1 **Put on your cycling shoes** and mark them on the outer side where your foot is widest. This point is usually slightly behind the smallest toe and is in line with the ball of the foot. The aim of setting up a cleat is to make sure that this part of your foot is exactly above the pedal axle when you ride.

4 **Put on your cycling shoes** and sit on your bike, engaging the cleats in the pedals.

● Ask someone to check from the side that the initial mark you made is over the pedal axle.

● Go for a ride and check whether your feet try to turn in or out on the pedals.

2 **Take off your shoes** and continue the mark you made with a straight line across the sole of your shoe, from outside to inside. This line must be at right angles to the initial mark and should end on the inner side of the shoe, in line with the initial mark.

3 **Place the cleat** on the shoe so that the line runs exactly through its center. Some cleats are marked to help with this alignment.

● Make sure that the horizontal axis of the cleat is exactly parallel with the line you made.

● Secure the cleat in place with the screws or Allen bolts provided.

5 **Adjust the cleats** to accommodate any foot position changes your test ride reveals, but keep the cleat centered over the axle.

● Mark the sole of your shoes all around the cleat, so that you can line it up again.

● Remove the cleat, put anti-seize compound on the screw threads, and line the cleat up with the marks you made. Tighten the cleat.

6 **Seal the Allen heads** on the bolts that secure the cleats to off-road shoes. These heads can fill with grit, causing them to lose shape and making it difficult to replace the cleats when they wear down. Prevent this by filling the Allen heads with blobs of a silicone sealant available from the hardware store.

STEERING AND

Steering gives you control of a bike's handling and direction. Regularly check and maintain the headset, handlebar, wheels, and hubs to safeguard their reliability at all times.

WHEELS

HEADSETS

A headset allows the bike to be steered. The headset must be properly adjusted to allow smooth, safe steering and to prolong its life. The bearings and bearing surfaces need regular inspection and lubrication, and anything that is worn must be replaced at once.

How they work

The main function of the headset is to enable the rider to change the direction of the front wheel under any conditions. There are two types of headsets, threaded and threadless, and both hold the front fork securely in the head tube, while simultaneously allowing the fork to turn freely.

   The headset rotates on bearings, which are held in place by cups, one above the head tube, the other below. For the forks to turn freely, these two cups press on the bearings just enough to prevent any play in the part of the fork known as the steerer tube. The way this pressure (also known as load) is achieved varies between the threaded and threadless headsets.

THREADLESS HEADSET ANATOMY

The stem cap bolt at the top of a threadless headset screws into a star washer below. Some types of threadless headsets contain a wedge instead of a star washer. When the stem cap bolt is turned with an Allen key, it pushes the stem and spacer down on to the bearings in both the top and bottom cups, and pulls up the steerer tube at the same time. This places sufficient load on the bearings for the fork to turn freely with no play. The stem is secured in place on the steerer by tightening two clamp bolts (not visible on the illustration).

Stem clamp bolts
Clamp stem to steerer tube

Stem cap bolt
Pulls the steerer tube upward

Star washer
Grips the steerer tube

Stem
Links handlebar and headset

Spacer
Sits on top of the bearings

Top bearings
Allow the steerer tube to turn in the headset

Top cup
Loads the bearings

Bottom cup
Loads the bearings

Steerer tube
Connects the fork to the headset

Bottom bearings
Allow the fork to turn

Fork crown
Turns the fork

THREADED HEADSET ANATOMY

Screwing the top cup down the thread of the steerer places a load on the top bearings to the point where the forks turn freely but without play. The cup, and consequently the front fork, is then locked in place by a lockring that also screws down the threaded steerer. The stem is attached to the headset by tightening the stem's expander bolt, which pulls up a wedge and jams the stem's quill inside the threaded steerer.

Stem
Links the handlebar and headset

Quill
Fits inside the threaded steerer

Expander bolt
Draws up the wedge

Lockring
Locks the top cup in place

Top bearings
Allow the steerer to turn in the headset

Top cup
Loads the bearings

Threaded steerer
Connects the headset to the fork

Wedge
Jams the quill in the steerer

Bottom bearings
Allow the fork to turn

Handlebar
Steers the front wheel

Headset
Holds the fork in the head tube

Fork
Holds and turns the front wheel

Steering effectively

A headset allows the rider to steer the front wheel effectively and confidently. The handlebar, which is connected to the steerer tube by the stem, turns the fork and the front wheel.

Threadless headset

To determine whether your bike is equipped with a threadless or a threaded headset, look at the stem. If you can see bolts on the side of the part that sits on top of the head tube, it is a threadless headset.

A number of different types of threadless headsets can be fitted to modern bikes. These range from the type that has both top and bottom cups, like the traditional headset, to others, such as the headset illustrated here, where the bearing surfaces fit inside the head tube. All the various types of headsets work on the same principle and are taken apart in a similar way.

Occasionally, you need to strip down the headset in order to check it for wear and to clean and lubricate the bearings. If you find any cups or bearing surfaces are worn, you will need to replace the whole headset. This job requires special equipment and is best left to the experts in a good bike shop.

STEP LOCATOR

Parts of a threadless headset

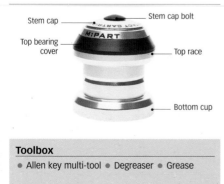

Stem cap — Stem cap bolt
Top bearing cover
Top race
Bottom cup

Toolbox
- Allen key multi-tool ● Degreaser ● Grease

Adjusting and cleaning a threadless headset

1 **Remove the stem cap bolt** from the center of the stem cap with an Allen key. This bolt loads the headset to prevent play in it, rather than securing the stem.

4 **Lower the fork** and lift off the top spacers and either the top cup or bearing cover, depending on the type of threadless headset.

● Clean, degrease, and look at the bottom bearing. If there are no signs of wear, grease the bearing.

● Take the centering wedge out of the head tube. Clean the bearings, bearing surfaces (*inset*), and bearing cover or top cup . Examine for wear, put new grease on the bearings, and reinstall.

2 **Loosen the clamp bolts** on the side of the stem once you have removed the cap bolt. The stem and handlebar assembly are now free. It is the stem clamp bolts that secure the stem to the steerer.

3 **Take hold of the front fork,** then lift the stem and handlebar from the steerer. You can leave these to hang out of the way, supported by the brake and gear cables.

5 **Put the fork back** into the head tube and replace the centering wedge, bearing cover, and spacers.

● Put the handlebar and stem back on top of the steerer.

● Load the headset by tightening the stem cap bolt to a point where the handlebar turns freely, but there is no play in the headset. Secure the stem in place by tightening the clamp bolts.

● Apply the front brake and try to push the bike forward to make sure the headset is not loose.

Threaded headset

Older bikes and children's bikes are equipped with threaded headsets. This type of headset is designed to make it easy to raise and lower the stem whenever you want to change the height of the handlebar and adjust your riding position.

The headset's top cup and the locknut that holds it in place are both screwed onto the steerer. The stem is equipped with a shaft, or quill, that fits inside the steerer. For safety reasons, you should never raise a stem above the limit marked on its quill.

On some even older headsets, the top cup screws down. Its serrated top edge is held in place by a clamp bolt on a similarly serrated lockring assembly. When the clamp bolt is loosened, the top cup screws off.

Remember to disconnect the brakes before you start working on the headset and make sure that you reconnect them when you are finished. Before the stem is replaced into the steerer of the headset, coat the quill with grease (see pp.30–1).

STEP LOCATOR

Parts of a threaded headset

- Spacer
- Locknut
- Top cup
- Top race
- SHIMANO ULTEGRA
- Bottom cup
- SHIMANO ULTEGRA
- Fork crown race

Toolbox

- 6mm Allen key • Grease • Degreaser • 30mm and 32mm headset wrenches • Plastic mallet

Servicing a threaded headset

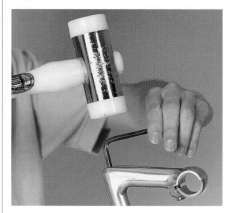

1 **Undo the Allen bolt** in the stem center and knock it downward with a plastic mallet to free the steerer. The stem is secured into the steerer by an expander bolt, which, as it is tightened, draws a wedge up inside the quill.

- Lift the stem from the steerer.

4 **Degrease all the bearing surfaces** of the top and bottom cups and of the races. You can access the top bearings by pushing the fork up the head tube and holding it there.

- Inspect the bearing surfaces. If any are damaged, you need a new headset; this is best left to a good bike shop.

2 **Unscrew the locknut** while holding the top cup still with a headset wrench.

● Spread newspaper on the floor to catch loose bearings that may drop out of the top cup.

● Lift off the spacers, then unscrew the top cup upward from the steerer.

3 **Lower the fork** to reveal the bearings in the bottom cup. Screwing the top cup upward allows this to happen. Although most headsets have ball bearings held in cages, watch out for loose bearings that may drop out of the bottom cup. Some headsets have roller bearings—treat these as ball bearings in the following steps.

5 **Grease both the top and bottom bearings** or set loose bearings in grease inside each cup.

● Completely unscrew the top cup to remove the bearings. Set the bearings individually in the greased cups and screw the top cup back on. Bearings held in cages can be greased in situ provided they are not worn out.

6 **Screw the top cup down** onto the top bearings. Replace the spacers and locknut.

● Adjust the top cup so that steering is free.

● Pull the fork to make sure there is no forward movement in the headset.

● Replace the spacer, hold the top cup with a wrench, and tighten the locknut onto it.

● Replace the stem and handlebar.

HANDLEBARS

Most modern bikes are equipped with either straight or drop handlebars. A rider must be able to rely totally on the handlebar, so for safety reasons, a handlebar must be replaced at once if scratches, stress marks, or cracks develop on the surface.

Straight handlebar

Owners of road bikes sometimes want to change the handlebar to a different shape, often to suit the proportions of their body or because of their cycling needs. Some cyclists want to replace a drop handlebar with a straight, or flat, bar. Others may want to replace their existing straight bars with riser bars, or vice versa. Riser bars, which are fitted to mountain bikes, are straight in the center, then rise up to become straight where the grips are. They are installed the same way as a straight handlebar.

The steps in this sequence apply to all straight handlebars, whatever the reason for replacing them. However, when replacing a drop handlebar with a straight bar, it will be necessary to swap the brake levers for levers that work with flat or riser bars. Some of these steps will also be useful when fitting new grips, brake levers, gear-shift levers, or bar-ends to an existing handlebar.

Parts of a straight handlebar

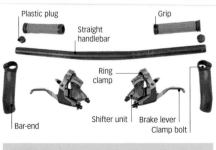

Plastic plug · Grip · Straight handlebar · Ring clamp · Bar-end · Shifter unit · Brake lever · Clamp bolt

Toolbox

- Half-round file • Emery paper • Ruler
- Allen key multi-tool • Hairspray

STEP LOCATOR

Installing a straight handlebar

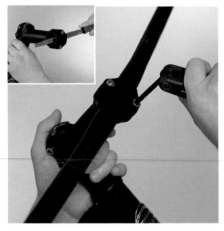

1 **Remove any raised pieces of metal** inside the stem clamp with a medium, half-round file (*inset*). Smooth the area with emery paper.

- Place the straight handlebar into the stem clamp and screw in the clamp bolts. Make sure the bar is centered before tightening it fully. If you are fitting a riser bar, decide what angle of sweep you want before tightening the bolts.

Secure the ring clamp of the brake lever to the handlebar. Like road brake levers, off-road levers have a ring clamp that fits over and secures them to the handlebar. Some off-road brake levers have integrated shift levers with only one clamp. However, some are separate and there are two clamps to go over the handlebar.

Spray hairspray into the handlebar grips to help the grips slide onto the handlebar. When the hairspray dries, the grips will fit tightly to the handlebars.

Slide the grips onto the handlebar while they are still wet with hairspray.

• Push the grips farther on if you are fitting bar-ends to allow for the width of the bar-end clamp.

• Fit grip-locks to hold the grips in place and prevent them from twisting while you are riding.

Clamp on the bar-ends. Line them up parallel with the angle of your stem to begin with, then adjust their angle to suit your own preference after riding.

• Put a plastic plug in each end of the handlebar to prevent injury in the event of a fall.

Drop handlebar

Road-riding cyclists often fit a drop handlebar to their bikes so their bodies can adopt a lower, more aerodynamic posture. However, the handlebar should never be positioned so low that breathing is restricted when holding the bottom of the bar.

Replace a drop handlebar at once if any cracks develop on its surface. The steps in this sequence will show how to replace a drop handlebar and how to fit, and therefore how to reposition, brake levers. Cyclists with larger hands and long arms may prefer to mount the levers lower down the handlebar than the ideal position shown here.

Regularly replace the handlebar tape as shown in Steps 5 and 6, and insert a plug in each end of the handlebar after taping to help prevent injury in a fall.

Brake levers for flat handlebars will not work on drop handlebars, and may not work with all brake types. Check the compatibility of your components before swapping.

STEP LOCATOR

1 2 3 4 5 6

Parts of a drop handlebar

Drop handlebar   Cable groove

Brake lever hood   Rubber cover   Handlebar tape   Brake lever

Toolbox
- Half-round file • Emery paper
- Allen key multi-tool

Installing a drop handlebar

1 **Use a medium, half-round file** to remove any raised areas of metal inside the part of the stem that clamps the bar in place. These raised areas can bite into the handlebar, eventually causing them to fracture.

- Smooth the filed surface with emery paper.

4 **Secure the levers** of a Campagnolo brake/shift to the handlebar by tightening a bolt on the outside of the hood with an Allen key. Pull the lever hood cover forward to access the bolt. The bolt on Shimano levers is farther down the outer side of the lever hood, so you need to put your Allen key into a recess under the rubber cover.

2 **Fit the new handlebar** and tighten up the clamp bolts. Before you secure the bolts, try to line up the flat part of the bottom of the handlebar with a point just below the back brake.

3 **Slide the steel ring** of the brake lever over the handlebar. This ring clamps the lever to the handlebar.

● Attach the bolt in the brake lever hood to the screw thread on the ring and tighten.

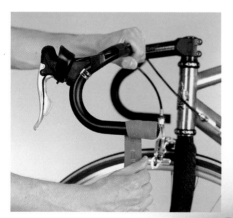

6 **Pull the cover** of the brake lever hood forward and place a short length of tape over each steel ring.

● Wind the tape in one turn from the bottom to the top of the lever hood. When you reach the top of the handlebar, secure the tape with electrical tape.

5 **Start taping** at one end of the handlebar.

● Wind upward, covering half of the previous turn with each subsequent turn.

● Keep the tape tight at all times.

HUBS

There are two types of hubs, open-bearing and cartridge. The cones and bearings of open-bearing hubs must be adjusted to let the hub spin freely, with little play. The bearings in both types of hubs need regular checking and lubricating.

How they work

The hub allows the wheel to revolve. Quick-release mechanisms or nuts secure the axle into the bike's frame. The axle remains static while the hub body spins around on bearings. Spokes run from the hub's flanges to the rim of the wheel—as the hub spins, so does the rim.

The drivetrain transfers the rider's power from the pedals to the rear wheel, while the front wheel is essentially pushed along by the revolutions of the rear. The gears on a bike are located on the rear hub, either as a hub-gear unit or as multiple cogs in the case of derailleur gears.

The freewheel mechanism, which is also on the rear hub, allows a rider to stop pedaling while the bike is in motion—for example, on a downhill stretch of road. This mechanism is part of the hub in both hub gears and hubs with cassette cogs.

Minimizing friction
Free-spinning hubs are an essential part of an efficient bike. Their bearings must create as little friction as possible, so as not to slow the rider's forward progress.

EXPLODED CARTRIDGE HUB

The axle of a cartridge hub is not threaded, so the bearings are pushed onto each end of the axle and covered by a seal. When the hub is assembled, the bearings sit in the hub body, just to the outside of the flanges, with the axle running through them. Lockrings ensure that everything is held in place.

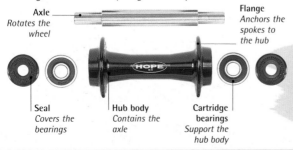

Axle
Rotates the wheel

Flange
Anchors the spokes to the hub

Seal
Covers the bearings

Hub body
Contains the axle

Cartridge bearings
Support the hub body

OPEN-BEARING FRONT HUB ANATOMY

The body on an open-bearing front hub spins on ball bearings that are set within, and at each end of, the hub body. Each set of bearings is held in place by a cone (not visible) that is screwed down on the thread at the end of the axle. A locknut (not visible) locks the cone in place on the same thread. If the hub is held by a quick-release mechanism, the axle is hollow to allow the quick-release skewer to go through it.

Axle
Remains static as the wheel revolves

Hub body
Rotates around the axle

Ball bearings
Support the hub body

Quick-release skewer
Locks the axle in place

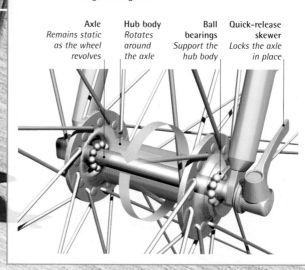

Open-bearing front hub
Allows the wheel to revolve smoothly

Open-bearing hub

Hubs are available in two types—open-bearing or cartridge. The open-bearing hubs require much more maintenance than the cartridge type, since their bearings need regular inspection, cleaning, and regreasing. As a result, the ability to strip down and service an open-bearing hub is a skill that can be used repeatedly.

The following steps will help you to remove an axle and a freehub, as well as regrease and retighten the bearings. They can be applied to a Shimano front or rear hub and a Campagnolo front hub. However, leave servicing a Campagnolo rear hub to the experts at a bike shop because it requires special tools.

If you are working on a rear hub, you need to remove the cassette by following the steps on *pp.66–7* before tackling the steps in this sequence.

STEP LOCATOR

Parts of an open-bearing hub

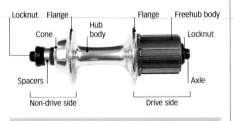

Locknut   Flange   Flange   Freehub body
              Hub body
Cone   Locknut

Spacers   Axle

Non-drive side   Drive side

Toolbox

- 15mm and 16mm cone wrenches (Shimano)
- 13mm and 14mm cone wrenches (Campagnolo)
- Grease • Grease gun (optional)
- Allen key multi-tool • Adjustable wrench
- 8mm or 10mm Allen key

Overhauling an open-bearing hub

1 **Remove the locknut** on the drive side with a wrench while holding the non-drive-side cone with a cone wrench. Some locknuts can be removed with an ordinary wrench, others with an Allen key.

- Keep holding the non-drive-side cone with the cone wrench and remove the drive-side cone with another cone wrench.

4 **Take out all the ball bearings** from each side and clean them with degreaser.

- Replace ball bearings that are scored or have flat spots on their surface.

- Insert a layer of grease into each groove, or race, where the ball bearings sit.

- Return the ball bearings to each race, pressing down firmly so the grease holds them in place.

2 **Pull the axle out** from the non-drive side. Be careful not to dislodge any of the ball bearings as you do so.

● Clean the cones and axle and then inspect them for damage. Check to see if the axle is bent by rolling it on a flat surface and looking for any irregular motion. Replace damaged cones or bent axles immediately.

3 **Insert an Allen key** into the 8mm or 10mm Allen bolt located in the center of the freehub. This bolt holds the freehub body on to the axle.

● Turn the key counterclockwise to remove the freehub. You may need a bit of force to loosen this bolt, so use an Allen key with a long handle for extra leverage.

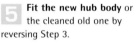

5 **Fit the new hub body** or the cleaned old one by reversing Step 3.

● Reinsert the axle from the non-drive side.

● Tighten the drive cone up to the bearings and make sure the axle spins freely with minimal play.

● Lock the cone into position with the locknut.

● Use the cone wrenches to check that the non-drive cone is tight against its locknut.

WHEELS

Quick-release mechanisms help to remove and replace a wheel more quickly than ever before. The tires are the component that make contact with the ground. Match the tires on your bike to the prevailing riding conditions and always be ready to replace worn-out tires.

Quick-release wheels

Removing and replacing a wheel is a very straightforward task, but if any of the following steps are overlooked, the wheel may come loose and compromise the rider's safety. The steps are for wheels that use quick-release levers to secure them in the dropout (the frame recess into which the axle fits). For bikes with axle nuts, loosening and tightening with a wrench corresponds to unlocking and locking the quick-release lever.

Levers are labeled "locked" or "closed" on the side facing the cyclist when the wheel is secure, and "unlocked" or "open" when it is not. Check levers are locked before each ride, and during a ride if disc brakes are fitted.

The rim brake needs to be released on the wheel being removed. For V-brakes, unhook the cable from its cradle; for cantilevers, unhook the straddle wire from the left brake arm; for calipers, use the quick-release lever.

Parts of the quick-release system

Fork

Quick-release lever

Quick-release body

Wheel dropout

Toolbox

● Wrenches for wheels with axle nuts

STEP LOCATOR

Removing a rear wheel

1 **Release the brake,** shift the chain onto the smallest cog, and pull the quick-release lever away from the bike into the unlocked position. Some quick-release levers are shaped so that they bend toward the frame when in the locked position. This provides a visual check if nothing is printed on the lever.

Removing a front wheel

1 **Release the brake.** Pull the quick-release lever to the unlocked position. If the dropout has safety lips, the wheel will not come out of the fork at this stage. These safety lips keep the wheel from falling out in the unlikely event of the lever becoming unlocked while you ride.

● Use your fingers to unscrew the nut on the opposite side of the lever until the quick-release clears the safety lip.

2 **Lift up the bike** to allow the wheel to drop out of the fork.

● Replace the front wheel by reversing Step 1.

● Push the quick-release lever behind the left fork blade to prevent anything from catching it and opening it accidentally.

● Reconnect the brake once the wheel is locked.

2 **Hook the chain** out of the way and onto the peg situated on the inner side of the right seat stay (if there is one).

● Pull the rear derailleur back and then lift up the rear of the bike.

● Give the tire a sharp blow from above with the heel of your hand if the wheel does not drop forward and out of the frame.

3 **Replace the wheel** by introducing the hub axle to the dropouts.

● Hook the chain onto the smallest cog, then push or pull the wheel backward.

● Line up the tire exactly in the middle of the chainstays as you hold the wheel straight.

● Push the quick-release lever into the locked position to secure the wheel. Reconnect the brake.

Puncture repair

When you are out on a ride, it is much easier to replace a punctured inner tube with an intact tube rather than painstakingly mend the puncture. At home, you can repair the punctured tube with adhesive and a patch. It is still a good idea to carry a repair kit on every ride, because you might be unlucky enough to get a second puncture and be forced to repair the tube outdoors.

The main point to remember about mending a puncture is not to rush any of the stages. If you patiently give the glue time to dry, closely examine the inside of the tire, and carefully refit the tube, then you will be rewarded with a successful repair. If you miss anything or pinch the inner tube, you may get another puncture.

STEP LOCATOR

1 2 3 4 5

Parts of a wheel

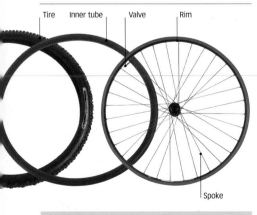

Tire   Inner tube   Valve   Rim

Spoke

Toolbox
- Tire levers ● Crayon ● Sandpaper ● Chalk
- Patch adhesive ● Repair patches

Mending a punctured inner tube

1 **Take the wheel out** of the bike. Place one tire lever under the tire bead and lift it off the rim. Hook this lever around one of the spokes.

● Insert another lever under the tire near the hooked lever. Push the second lever forward and run it around the whole circumference of the rim to remove one side of the tire.

● Remove the inner tube from the rim.

4 **Take the tire off the wheel,** turn it inside out, and thoroughly check the inner surface.

● Remove anything that is sticking through the tire by pulling it out from the outside of the tire.

2 **Inflate the tube** a little and listen for the sound of escaping air. Locate the hole, mark it with a crayon, and let the air out of the tube.

● Spread a thin layer of adhesive over and around the hole (*inset*). Allow time for it to become tacky.

● Peel the foil from the patch. Press the patch firmly onto the adhesive for over a minute. Make sure the edges are flat.

3 **Use a small piece of sandpaper** to dust some chalk over the patch to prevent excess adhesive from sticking to the inside of the tire.

● Leave the tube for a few minutes to make sure that the adhesive has dried.

5 **Put one side of the tire** all the way back onto the rim. Slightly inflate the tube, insert the valve into the hole in the rim, and work the tube back inside the tire.

● Put the other side of the tire in place by pushing the valve upward, then lifting the section of tire next to the valve over the rim. Work the tire back around the rim.

● Check that the tire has not pinched the tube underneath it before fully inflating the tube. To do this, squeeze the tire together and look around the whole circumference of the wheel.

Spokes and rims

The steps in this sequence explain how to replace a single broken spoke and how to true a wheel, a term for straightening the rim of a wheel. However, replacing multiple spokes, replacing spokes in nonstandard wheels, and truing a wheel that has been buckled by some kind of impact are jobs that are best left to the experts in a good bike repair shop.

It is essential to true the wheel after replacing a broken spoke because the wheel rim is kept straight by the combined pull of all the spokes acting on it. If one spoke breaks, its pull is eliminated and the rim as a whole goes out of line.

A wheel jig is needed to true a wheel properly. This tool holds the wheel securely in place, and its jaws provide a reference point on either side of the rim to help judge how far out of line the wheel is. Bringing it in line is a matter of tightening the new spoke until it reaches the same tension as the old spoke.

STEP LOCATOR

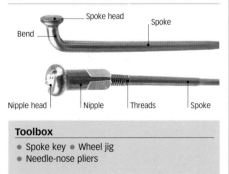

Parts of a spoke

Spoke head — Spoke

Bend

Nipple head | Nipple | Threads | Spoke

Toolbox

- Spoke key ● Wheel jig
- Needle-nose pliers

Replacing a spoke and truing a wheel

1 Remove the wheel and take off the tire and inner tube.

● Lift up the rim tape next to the broken spoke and push the spoke upward and out of the rim. If the head of the spoke is broken, measure the broken spoke so you can buy the correct length to replace it. If the break occurred in another place, measure the two pieces to get the right length.

4 Screw the nipple onto the spoke. For the first few turns you can use your fingers.

● Go back to Step 2 and make sure it is laced exactly the same way as the spoke four along from it. If it is not laced properly, tensioning the spoke in Steps 5 and 6 could damage the wheel.

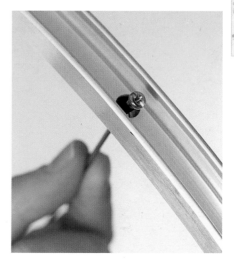

2 **Insert the new spoke,** threads first, into the hub flange from the opposite side from its two neighbors.

● Lace the new spoke into the wheel, under and over the neighboring spokes. To do this, look at the spoke four along and lace the new spoke exactly the same way.

3 **Push the nipple** of the new spoke through the rim hole from inside the rim and screw it onto the spoke.

● Remove the rim tape to make it easier to fit the nipple onto the new spoke.

● Check the rim tape—if you see any splits, or if it is frayed, replace the tape.

5 **Put the wheel into a wheel jig** and take up the remaining slack on the spoke nipple by tightening it with a spoke key. Make sure that the spoke key is precisely the right size for the nipples on the wheel.

● Stop short of making the spoke as tight as its neighbors at this stage.

6 **Use small, measured turns** of the spoke key to tension the spoke.

● Rotate the wheel so that the nipple of the new spoke is between the jaws of your jig.

● Note how out of line the rim is, then give the nipple a one-quarter tightening turn and check again between the jaws. Repeat and check each quarter-turn until the rim is straight.

ADJUSTING YOUR

BRAKES

Trustworthy brakes are a bike's most important component. The braking system needs to be adjusted and serviced carefully and precisely to guarantee a rider's safety in all conditions.

RIM BRAKES

Rim brakes stop a bike by contacting the rim of the wheels. Pads must be checked to ensure that they contact the rim fully and at the same time, and replaced when they are worn. Brake cables must be checked and lubricated regularly.

How they work

The three most common types of rim brake—V-brake, cantilever, and caliper—work in similar ways. A lever pulls a cable, which causes the two brake arms to move toward each other simultaneously. This action brings the two pads into contact with the braking surface of the wheel rim. Springs cause the arms to move back when the lever is released. Cantilever brakes distribute the cable's pull via a straddle wire. The inner cable in a V-brake and caliper pulls one arm, while the outer, in resisting this pull, effectively pushes the other arm.

Braking safely
Rim brakes must be set up properly and maintained to very high standards if they are to work effectively and safely on any surface and in all conditions.

V-BRAKE ANATOMY

The cable of a V-brake is attached to a brake arm by a cable-clamp bolt. When pulled, the cable pulls this arm toward the rim. At the same time, the cable-guide tube, which is an extension of the cable housing, pushes the other arm inward. The two arms pivot around the brake bosses, pushing the brake pads against the braking surface on the rim. Once the cable's pull is released, springs around the pivot bolts push the brake arms apart.

Cable-guide tube
Pushes the brake arm

Brake arm
Pivots inward on a brake boss

Inner cable
Pulls the brake arm

Cable-clamp bolt
Attaches the cable to the brake arm

Brake boss
Allows the brake arm to pivot

Brake pad
Contacts the rim and stops the wheel

Springs
Push brake arms apart

Pivot bolt
Anchors the brake arm to the brake boss

Brake lever
Pulls the cable

Brake arm
Moves the brake pads toward the rim

Brake pad
Slows down the wheel

BRAKE LEVER ANATOMY

When the rider applies the brake lever, it pulls the nipple of the inner cable. As it leaves the lever, the brake cable runs inside a cable housing, which sits in a barrel adjuster. This barrel adjuster allows the brake travel to be fine-tuned.

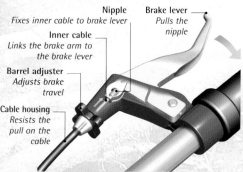

Nipple
Fixes inner cable to brake lever

Brake lever
Pulls the nipple

Inner cable
Links the brake arm to the brake lever

Barrel adjuster
Adjusts brake travel

Cable housing
Resists the pull on the cable

Drop handlebar brake cable

Brake cables on a drop handlebar need to be changed at regular intervals, although this depends on how much the road bike is used. For a heavily used bike, change the brake cables every two months; for a bike ridden lightly two or three times a week, change the brake cables once a year.

The steps in this sequence are performed on the back brake. Replacing a cable on the front brake follows the same principles, but there are no cable guides to thread through.

Brake levers that fit a drop handlebar require a brake cable with a pear nipple. Always keep a new cable in the toolbox or workshop as a spare. A rear cable can be cut to fit the front as well. Once the cable has been removed, remember to put a few drops of lubricant on the pivots around which the brake lever moves, and spray some oil into the tube inside the lever hood where the cable is inserted.

STEP LOCATOR

Parts of a brake lever and brake cable

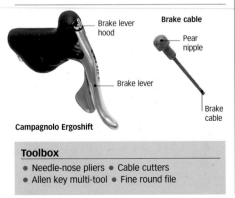

Brake lever hood

Brake cable

Pear nipple

Brake lever

Brake cable

Campagnolo Ergoshift

Toolbox
- Needle-nose pliers • Cable cutters
- Allen key multi-tool • Fine round file

Replacing road bike brake cables

1 **Loosen the cable-clamp bolt** on the brake caliper. Remove the old cable by pulling its nipple from the lever hood with needle-nose pliers.

- Note exactly where the cable fits in the lever hood to allow you to fit the new one easily.

- If the old cable has broken, remove the part of the cable that is still clamped to the calliper.

- Carefully unwind the handlebar tape.

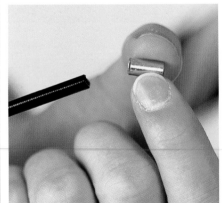

4 **Fit each length** of cable housing with a metal ferrule at both ends. When you apply the brake, ferrules prevent the cable housings from being pulled through the cable guides on the frame.

- Make sure that each ferrule is pushed all the way on. Put a little oil on the end of the ferrule to help it slide into place, and wipe off any excess.

2 **Insert the new, greased cable** into the cradle on the lever in which the nipple sits.

● Thread the cable into the tube in the lever hood. Push it in and watch for it to come out of the back of the lever hood. Now pull it through the lever hood from behind.

● Make sure that the nipple is seated in the brake lever cradle when the cable is all the way through.

3 **Cut the new cable housing to length** with good-quality cable cutters. Measure the old housing and cut the new one to the same length.

● Always cut between the spirals of the housing.

● Dribble oil into the housing, holding it while the oil runs down to coat the inside.

● Renew cable housings at regular intervals.

5 **Thread the cable** through the first length of cable housing and the first cable guide.

● Pull the cable all the way through and insert it into the next guide, then the next housing.

● Push the cable housings firmly into the guides to ensure there is no slack when applying the brakes.

● Use a fine round file to file out any tight cable guides. Do not file more than you have to.

6 **Pull the cable** through the cable-clamp bolt on the caliper until each brake pad is about 2mm from the wheel rim.

● Hold the cable and tighten the clamp bolt. If the brake has a quick release, ensure that it is in the closed position before tightening the clamp bolt.

● Follow Steps 5 and 6 on p.97 to re-tape the handlebar, with either new or existing tape.

Straight handlebar brake cable

Replacing brake cable inners and housings is a job that should be done fairly often on a mountain bike—about once every six to 12 months. They also need replacing if they start fraying and become worn. The hybrid bike in this sequence has V-brakes, but some mountain bikes are equipped with cantilever brakes. Fitting cables is similar for both.

Brake cables also require regular cleaning and lubricating, especially if the bike has been ridden consistently in wet weather. All brake levers that fit onto a straight or riser handlebar require a cable with a barrel nipple.

Regardless of the manufacturer, the barrel nipple fits into the brake lever in the same way. Remember to use ferrules on both ends of every length of new cable housing. Put a cable crimp on the end of the cable once everything is secure and working as it should.

In these steps, the tire is removed from the wheel to show clearly what is happening.

STEP LOCATOR

Parts of a brake lever and a brake cable

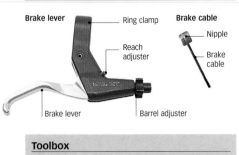

Brake lever   Ring clamp   **Brake cable**

Reach adjuster   Nipple

Brake cable

Brake lever   Barrel adjuster

Toolbox

- Needle-nose pliers • Cable cutters
- Allen key multi-tool • Cable pullers (optional)

Replacing V-brake cables on a hybrid bike

1 **Undo the cable–clamp bolt** on the brake. Note where the nipple sits in the cradle that is part of the lever and remove the cable from inside the brake lever by pulling it out with needle-nose pliers.

● Check the cable housings. If they are not worn, you can use them again. Flush them out with degreaser and dribble oil into them.

4 **Attach the cable** to the brake arm by inserting it into the cable guide tube and then pull it through the cable-clamp bolt.

● Keep the cable under tension and make sure each length of cable housing is properly seated in the cable guides.

● Pull the cable to bring the brake pads closer to the rim. Tighten the clamp bolt when the pads are about 2mm from the rim.

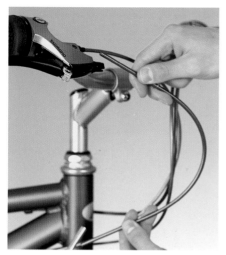

2 **Cut new cable housings** to the same length as the housings you removed, or measure them on your bike and trim as needed. Buy cable housing either in a roll or in precut lengths with inners in a cable kit. The precut lengths may be too long for your bike, so you may still have to cut to fit.

● Dribble oil into each cable housing and push a metal ferrule onto each end.

3 **Grease the new inner** and thread it into the brake lever. When it shows through the barrel adjuster, pull it from this side of the lever until the nipple is seated in the lever cradle.

● Thread the cable through the lengths of cable housing and seat the cable housings in the cable guides of the frame.

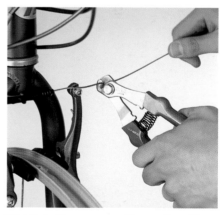

5 **Pull the brake lever** until the brake is fully applied. This ensures that all cable housings are bedded in and all bolts are tight.

● Undo the cable-clamp bolt and repeat Step 4 if the cable slips through the clamp bolt or a ferrule is not seated properly.

6 **Cut off any excess cable** once the cables are bedded in.

● Leave about 1½in (4cm) of free cable after the cable-clamp bolt.

● Put a cable crimp on the end of the cable to prevent it from fraying.

Caliper brake

Maintaining caliper brakes is a question of regularly checking the action of the brake lever. If you have to pull it too far before the brake bites, the brake needs adjusting. Check the brake pads for wear and alignment, and ensure that they contact the braking surface of the rims simultaneously.

How far the lever has to be pulled before the brake comes on depends on the rider. People with smaller hands may prefer more travel in the lever before the brake bites, because they will pull with more strength the closer the lever is to the handlebar.

Apart from their quick releases, all dual-pivot caliper brakes (such as the Shimano brakes shown here) work in the same way, regardless of the manufacturer. This means that you should be able to apply these steps to your bike, whatever its brakes.

STEP LOCATOR

Parts of a caliper brake

Travel adjuster, spring, and washer

Caliper arm

Center-fixing bolt

Centering adjusting screw

ULTEGRA

Brake shoe bolt

Brake pad

Brake shoe

Toolbox

- Full set of Allen keys or Allen key multi-tool
- Needle-nose pliers (optional)

Adjusting a caliper brake

1 **Periodically check for pad wear.** If the pads are wearing down toward half their original depth, they must be replaced.

- Undo the Allen key pad retainer and push out the pad. If the pad and shoe are a complete piece, replace the whole unit, releasing the old pad and fitting the new one with a 5mm Allen key.

3 **Pull the brake on** with the brake lever and check to see if both pads simultaneously come in contact with the braking surface on the rim of the wheel.

- Make sure that both sides are working together by turning an adjustment screw on the side of the caliper with an Allen key. This process is called "centering" the brakes.

Using quick-release mechanisms

2 **Adjust the brake pads** so they are directly in line with the braking surface of the rim.

● Release the 5mm Allen bolt on the pad and line the pad up with the braking surface.

● Look for pad wear at this point. Pads that have been set too low will develop a lip and will need to be replaced.

1 **Use a quick-release mechanism** when the adjusted brake pads are so close to the rim that it is impossible to remove the wheel. Campagnolo and Shimano caliper brakes are equipped with different quick-release systems.

● Lift the small lever on the cable-fixing bolt to make Shimano caliper brake pads move away from the rim. After replacing the wheel, lower the lever.

4 **Adjust the brake travel** if you have to pull the brake lever back a long way toward the handlebar before the wheel stops moving.

● Undo the cable-fixing bolt and squeeze the sides of the caliper until the pads nearly touch the rim. The brake cable will then move through the fixing bolt.

● Tighten the bolt and release the caliper.

1 **Press the small button** at the side of the brake lever to move Campagnolo caliper brake pads away from the rim.

● Restore the pads to their original position by pulling the brake lever toward the handlebar until the brakes are on and then push the small button back.

V-brake

V-brakes are fitted to most new mountain bikes because they give good stopping power. Maintaining brake performance is crucial because of the harsh conditions to which mountain bikes are sometimes subjected, so knowing how to adjust the brakes at home and out on the trail is very important.

Pad alignment and brake travel need to be checked and adjusted regularly to keep them working properly. Bear in mind that as soon as you ride off-road you will increase brake pad wear. Even a single ride can render already worn pads useless, so change them before they need it.

Adjustment in the workshop, especially pad alignment, is best performed with the tire removed, since off-road tires are bulky and can get in the way. Wheels must run true before setting up brakes (*see pp.106–7*).

STEP LOCATOR

Parts of a V-brake

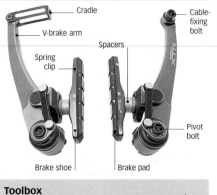

Cradle
V-brake arm
Spacers
Cable-fixing bolt
Spring clip
Pivot bolt
Brake shoe
Brake pad

Toolbox

● Full set of Allen keys or Allen key multi-tool
● Phillips screwdriver ● Cable puller (optional)

Adjusting a V-brake

1 **Make sure the stopper pin** on each brake arm is seated in the same hole on the brake bosses. If it is not, remove the pivot bolt, slide the brake arm off the boss, and put the pin into the correct hole.

● Replace the pivot bolt and retighten it. If you notice that the brake boss was dry with the arm removed, smear a little grease on it.

4 **Retension the brakes** by hooking the cable back in its cradle.

● Make sure the gap between each brake pad and the rim of the wheel is 1mm.

● Undo the cable-fixing bolt with an Allen key and pull the cable through until the 1mm gap is achieved. Then tighten the cable-fixing bolt.

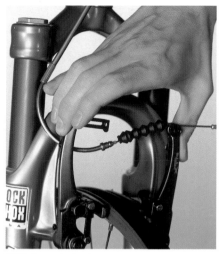

2 **Press the brake arms together**. If they are not vertical when the pads touch the rim, rearrange the spacers on either side of the pads until they are vertical.

- Release the brakes by unhooking the cable-guide tube from the cradle. Do this when you remove the wheel with correctly adjusted V-brakes.

3 **Undo the brake–pad fixing bolt**, remove the pad and shoe assembly, and switch the spacers around.

- Check the pads. If they are worn, remove the pad-retaining clip, push the old pad out of the shoe, and replace it with a new one.

- Line up the pads so that they hit the rim with their entire braking surface, and are parallel to it. Then tighten the fixing bolts.

5 **Use a Phillips screwdriver** to tighten or loosen the centering screw on each brake arm. The aim is to make both arms move an equal distance before the pad touches the rim when you apply the brake lever.

- The tension on each screw should ideally be even, since there is an equal number of spacers on either side of the brake arm.

6 **Screw out the barrel adjuster** on the brake lever to reduce brake travel and make the brakes feel more responsive.

- Screw the adjuster outward to reduce brake travel and create firmer braking. This technique is quick and easy to perform, and is especially useful for riding in wet conditions, when brake pads can wear down rapidly.

Cantilever brake

Cantilever brakes work with the brake levers that fit dropped handlebars, whereas V-brakes do not. This is why touring and cyclo-cross bikes are fitted with cantilevers. Cantilevers were the predecessors of V-brakes, so they may also be fitted to older mountain and hybrid bikes.

Keep cantilever brakes running smoothly by regularly checking the pads for wear and adjusting the pad alignment and brake travel.

The cable of the cantilever brake shown in these steps is clamped to one brake arm and the straddle wire running off it attaches to the other arm. On some older cantilever brakes, the brake cable is attached to a straddle. This hooks the straddle wire that transfers the cable's pull to both brake arms and needs regular adjustment (*see Step 1 Adjusting a BMX U-brake, pp.122–23*).

STEP LOCATOR

Parts of a cantilever brake

Brake shoe   Brake pad
Cantilever arm   Cable-clamp bolt
Spring clip
Brake pad Allen nut   Spacers

Toolbox

- 5mm Allen key ● Grease gun (optional)
- Grease

Adjusting a cantilever brake

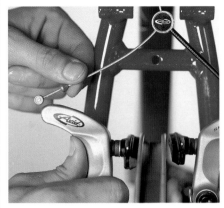

1 **Disconnect the straddle wire** by pushing the cantilever arm to which it is attached toward the wheel with one hand. At the same time, unhook the nipple on the straddle with the other hand.

- Undo the pivot bolts that attach the cantilever arms to the frame bosses.
- Remove the cantilever arms.

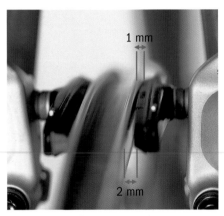

1 mm

2 mm

4 **Angle the pads** so that the front of each pad hits the rim before the rear when the brakes are applied—this is called "toe in."

- Loosen the pad-fixing bolt and place an emery board between the rear of the pad and the rim. Apply the brakes and then tighten the bolt. Release the brakes and remove the emery board. Ideally, the front of the pad should be 1mm from the rim and the rear 2mm.

2 **Clean the exposed frame bosses** with a cloth soaked in degreaser, then lubricate with a light grease, not a heavy-duty industrial grease. Use a grease gun if you have one.

● Bolt both arms back on to the bosses, making sure that the stopper pins are inserted into the same hole on each boss.

● Replace the pivot bolts and then tighten them to hold the brake arms to the bosses.

3 **Check the pads.** If one is worn or badly aligned, undo the pad-fixing bolt with an Allen key and remove the pad/shoe assembly.

● Remove the spring clip from the brake shoe and slide out the worn pad. Slide in a new pad and replace the spring clip.

● Return the assembly to the brake arm, line up the pad so that its entire surface contacts the rim and is parallel with it, then tighten the bolt.

5 **Undo the brake–cable clamp** to achieve the proper spacing from the pad to the rim.

● Pull the cable through the clamp until the front of each brake pad is 1mm from the rim. Tighten the clamp bolt.

● Pull the brake lever to see if both brake arms contact the rim simultaneously. If they do not, screw the centering screws in or out on each arm until they do.

Alternative brake designs

Two alternative brake designs are commonly fitted to some new bikes. These are the side-pull caliper brakes used on children's bikes and the U-brakes fitted on BMX bikes. Side-pulls work in much the same way as calipers (see pp.116–17), while U-brakes resemble cantilevers (see pp.120–21).

Before buying replacement cables for either of these types of brakes, first check the kind of nipple that is currently used on the bike in question. Some levers on children's bikes and older bikes require pear nipples, while other levers need barrel nipples. When a new cable is fitted to a side-pull caliper brake, leave the barrel adjuster at the halfway point of its range.

STEP LOCATOR

Parts of a side-pull brake and a U-brake

Side-pull caliper brake — Barrel adjuster

Pivot nut

Brake arms — Cable-clamp bolt

Brake pad — Brake-pad bolt

BMX U-brake

Straddle-clamp bolt — Pivot bolts — Straddle-wire seat — Centering screw

Brake arms

Brake-pad bolt — Brake pads

Toolbox

- Allen key multi-tool ● Needle-nose pliers
- Wrenches

Adjusting a side-pull caliper brake

1 **Loosen the cable–clamp bolt** and pull the cable through until the brake pads are closer to the rim. This compensates for pad wear.

- Screw in the barrel adjuster to move the pads away or screw it out to move them closer.

- Replace pads that are worn below half their depth by undoing the pad bolt and fitting a new pad or shoe unit in their place.

Adjusting a BMX U-brake

1 **Undo the straddle clamp** bolt and pull the brake cable through the straddle with needle-nose pliers to take up the pad wear. Then tighten the nut.

2 **Use an Allen key** to adjust the centering screw on each brake arm if the pads do not contact the rim at the same time. Screw in to move the pad away from the rim.

2 **Center the brakes** if one brake pad is contacting the rim before the other.

● Undo the brake's pivot nut that holds it in place and is located behind the fork crown.

● Hold the caliper so that both pads are an equal distance from the rim and tighten the pivot nut.

3 **Undo the pad bolts,** line up the pads, and tighten the bolt so that the brake pads contact the rim directly in line with it. Do this when you replace worn pads, too.

● Inspect the pads regularly. If you find any ridges on them, replace the pads (*see Step 1*) and then line them up as described above, so that their entire surface contacts the rim.

3 **Line up or replace pads** in the same way as caliper brakes (*see pp.116–17*). Replace the brake pads by removing the pad bolts and fitting new pad and shoe units.

● To disconnect the brake, pinch the brake arms together and unhook the straddle from the straddle wire. To reconnect, reverse this procedure.

HUB-MOUNTED BRAKES

Hub-mounted brakes stop a bike by slowing down the speed of the hub. Regularly check disc brake pads for wear and alignment, replacing them when they are worn. Regularly check and replace the cables on cable discs and hub brakes. Examine the hoses of hydraulic brakes for leaks.

How they work

Hub-mounted brakes are activated by the pull of a lever on a cable, which causes pads to contact a braking surface. Springs push the pads away when the lever is released. In disc brakes, the pads act on discs attached to the hub.

In roller and coaster brakes, the pads act on a braking surface inside the hub. The action of the pads on the surface then slows down the hub and therefore the wheel. In hydraulic brakes, the lever's action pushes fluid through a hose; this fluid pushes the brake pads in the caliper into action. Of all the hub-mounted brakes, hydraulic disc brakes offer a rider the best control over the braking forces that can be applied.

Working in any weather
An advantage of hub brakes over rim brakes is that their performance is largely unaffected by adverse riding conditions.

HYDRAULIC DISC BRAKE ANATOMY

When the rider pulls the brake lever, the hydraulic fluid in the hose pushes on the pistons in the caliper. These pistons in turn cause the brake pad on each side of the disc to contact the disc and slow the rotation of the wheel. When the rider releases the brake lever, the pressure of the fluid in the hose decreases, allowing the springs (not visible) in the caliper to push the brake pads apart.

Hose
Contains fluid

Caliper
Contains pistons and two brake pads

Brake pad
Contacts the disc under pressure from the fluid

Disc
Slows down the hub of the wheel under pressure from the brake pads

Hose
Carries the brake fluid from the lever to the caliper

Brake lever
Compresses the brake fluid

HYDRAULIC BRAKE LEVER

Brake hoses are connected to a reservoir of brake fluid on each brake lever. The fluid fills the hoses all the way to the caliper on the wheel. Pulling the brake lever operates a piston in the reservoir, which pushes the fluid down the hose and, as a result, activates the caliper pistons.

Caliper
Houses the braking mechanism

Disc
Slows down the wheel

Replacing disc brake pads

When brake pads wear down, the brakes will not stop the wheel as quickly. Eventually, the pads become so worn that they have to be replaced. Unevenly worn pads should also be replaced immediately and the caliper may need to be realigned (*see p.129*).

Although replacing pads is broadly the same for all makes and models of disc brake, there are some differences, mostly in the way the pads are retained within the brake caliper. Some brake pads are kept in position within the caliper by retaining bolts, while others rely on the spring that keeps the two pads apart to fix them in place.

Only use replacement pads recommended by the manufacturer of your brakes, and be very careful how you handle the pads.

STEP LOCATOR

Parts of a disc-brake caliper

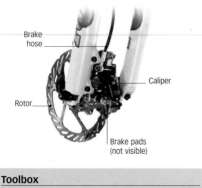

Brake hose

Caliper

Rotor

Brake pads (not visible)

Toolbox

- Allen keys or Allen key multi-tool
- Flat-bladed screwdriver

Changing the pads

1 **Remove the wheel from the frame** or forks (*see pp.102–3*), depending on which brake you are working on.

● Taking care not to touch the disc brake rotor, lower the wheel from the bike by supporting it with both hands on the axle, on each side of the hub.

● If you do touch a rotor you must clean it, or the performance of the brake will be reduced (*see pp.128–29*).

4 **Place the new pads on either side** of the spring, which is V-shaped when looked at from the side. The tabs of the pads should be at the open end of the V. The narrowest part of the V goes into the caliper first.

● Taking care not to touch the pad surface, hold the pad and spring assembly between the thumb and forefinger, ready to put it in the caliper.

Remove the pad from the caliper. The pads on this model are held in place within the caliper by outward pressure from a spring.

• Before you can push the pads out, you need to prise them apart with a flat-bladed screwdriver.

• If your brakes have a mechanism for taking up pad wear you need to fully wind it out.

• If your bike has a pad-retaining bolt, remove it with an Allen key.

Once the pads are dislodged, and all internal pressure is off them, squeeze them together. Use the tabs at the front of the pads to pull them free from the caliper. Sometimes they need a gentle push from behind with a flat-bladed screwdriver.

• If you have to push them, take each pad out separately and ensure that the separating spring comes out, too.

Squeeze the pad/spring assembly together and push it into the open end of the caliper. Slide the assembly all the way in, listening for the "click" sound that indicates it is seated correctly in the caliper. Let go once you hear the "click."

• The pads should separate when you let go of them. If they don't, remove and reassemble them, then push them in again, repeating Steps 2–5.

Put the wheel back in the frame or fork, ensuring the quick-release lever is locked.

• Bed the pads in by spinning the wheel and pulling the brake lever a number of times. Ride the bike for a short time to test the brakes fully.

• Some brakes have micro-adjusters for fine-tuning their action—adjust this feature if present on your brakes.

Disc-brake care

Cable disc brakes work well in all conditions. Even so, check the brake cables regularly for signs of fraying and keep them well lubricated. If the brakes do not release quickly when you let go of the brake lever, they need to be lubricated. Check brake travel, too, since excessive travel can mean that the brake pads are worn.

When lubricating your bike, make sure that the lubricant does not fall on or touch the brake discs or pads. Do not even touch the disc or pad faces, because the grease from your fingers can easily affect their performance. Always clean the discs with a specialized rotor-cleaning fluid.

Check your disc brake rotors regularly for accuracy and cracks, and clean them after every ride to ensure good brake performance. Replace a cracked or buckled rotor at once.

STEP LOCATOR

Parts of a cable disc brake (front)

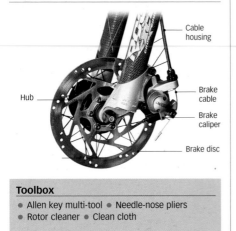

Cable housing

Hub

Brake cable

Brake caliper

Brake disc

Toolbox
- Allen key multi-tool • Needle-nose pliers
- Rotor cleaner • Clean cloth

Adjusting cable travel

1 **Loosen the cable-clamp bolt** on the caliper and pull through enough cable, with pliers or a cable-pulling tool, to take up any slack in the cable.

• Tighten the clamp bolt. This will reduce the travel on the brakes and is a necessary adjustment if the brake levers need to be pulled a long way before the brakes work.

Looking after rotors

1 **Check the rotor for accuracy** by inspecting how it moves through the calliper when the wheel is turned. It should run absolutely straight and true.

• Spin the wheel quickly, but ensure you are holding your bike steady.

2 **Screw out the barrel adjuster** to reduce brake travel. The adjuster is just above where the cable housing sits on the caliper body.

● Loosen the fixing clamp to remove the old cable if a new cable is needed. Insert the new cable into the brake lever (see pp.114–15) and follow Steps 1 and 2 with the new cable.

● Lubricate the new cable before you fit it.

3 **Align the calipers** with the discs using the adjustment bolts. Undo these bolts, align the caliper so that its sides are parallel with the disc, and then tighten.

● Align brakes that are not equipped with this adjustment facility by using spacers to pack out the caliper-fixing bolts.

2 **Remove a cracked or buckled rotor** by unscrewing the bolts, holding it to the hub with an Allen key. Replace it with the specific rotor for your type of brake.

● Place the new rotor over the threaded bolt holes in the hub. Screw in and tighten the bolts.

3 **Clean the rotor** with a special rotor-cleaning fluid after removing the wheel.

● Spray a little cleaner on either side of the rotor.

● Use a clean cloth to prevent the cleaner from coating other bike parts but also to ensure the rotor is covered with cleaner. Do not polish with it.

Hydraulic disc brake I

Hydraulic disc brakes are more powerful than cable disc brakes, and once correctly installed, will require less maintenance. A bike that has disc-brake mountings on the frame and fork will be suitable for a disc-brake system.

Cable disc brakes can work with rim-brake levers but their performance falls fractionally short of hydraulic systems. These work by compressing a fluid rather than pulling a cable. Compatible hydraulic brake levers will need to be fitted to the handlebar and brake hoses that hold the brake fluid. Disc-specific hubs will also be required.

There is no need to fasten the front hose to the fork. To direct and keep the rear hose in place, use an adapter kit to let the frame's cable guides take hoses, because the cable hole in a standard cable guide is too small.

STEP LOCATOR

Parts of a hydraulic disc brake

- Caliper
- Hose
- Wheel quick-release
- Disc bolt
- Disc

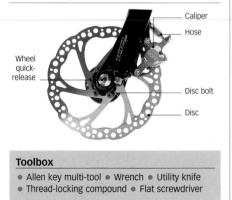

Toolbox

- Allen key multi-tool ● Wrench ● Utility knife
- Thread-locking compound ● Flat screwdriver

Installing a hydraulic disc-brake system

1 **Fit the caliper** using the Allen bolts and washers provided.

- Switch the washers around to pack out each caliper in order to line it up with the disc.

- Apply a thread-locking compound to the threads, then fix the disc to the hub using the disc bolts.

2 **Cut the hose** of the hydraulic system if it is too long by following Steps 3–7.

● Take out the brake pads (*see pp.126–7*) first and replace them with a spacer. The caliper used here is a demonstration model with no hose attached.

3 **Mount the brake lever** onto the handlebar and secure with the clamp bolts.

● Unscrew the aluminum shroud located where the hose joins the brake lever and move it out of the way. Pry open the brass olive beneath with a flat screwdriver.

4 **Move the brass olive** along the hose and out of the way.

● Pry the hose off the brake lever joint with a flat screwdriver, but be careful not to damage the lever joint. At the same time, gently pull on the hose to detach it.

5 **Carefully cut off** excess cable from the detached end of the hose with a sharp knife. Keep the olive and the shroud on the part of the hose that you will be reconnecting.

6 **Join the hose** to the brake lever by inserting it into the lever joint. Push it home firmly, but not too hard, since this can split the hose.

● Hold the hose upward as you work to keep brake fluid loss to a minimum.

7 **Squeeze the olive** on to the hose at the lever joint to make a good seal.

● Screw the shroud on to the thread of the lever joint.

● Bleed the disc-brake system (*see pp.132–3*).

Hydraulic disc brake II

If you are pulling hard on the brake levers without much effect on the discs, or if you are pulling the levers several times to make the brakes work, you need to bleed air from the system. The following steps will also help if you have cut hoses to fit while installing a hydraulic system, had a leak in the system, or have fitted a new hose.

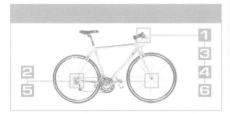

Toolbox

- Allen key multi-tool • 10mm wrench
- Length of clear hose

Draining and replacing brake fluid

1 **Remove the wheels** from the bike to reduce the chance of brake fluid falling on the brake discs.

- Place a spacer in the caliper between the brake pads (*see Step 2, p.131*).

- Take off the brake fluid reservoir cover on the brake lever with an Allen key. Be careful not to let any of the brake fluid touch your hands.

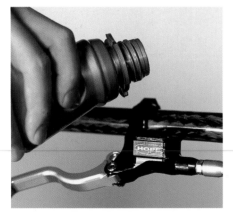

4 **Angle the bike** so that the reservoir is level, open the bleed nipple, and fill the reservoir with brake fluid. Pour with a smooth, constant stream to minimize air bubbles.

- Squeeze the brake lever all the way to the handlebar and hold it. Close the bleed nipple.

- Never mix brake fluids. Mineral oil or DOT 4 fluids cannot be interchanged.

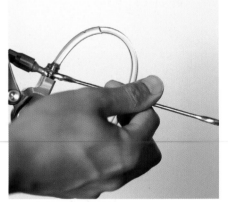

5 **Repeat Step 4,** filling up the reservoir until there are no more air bubbles flowing through the clear tube when you squeeze the brake lever. You will probably have to repeat this step four or five times before the bubbles in the tube completely disappear.

- Close the bleed nipple once the tube is bubble-free and the reservoir is full.

2 **Open the bleed nipple** on the caliper with a 10mm wrench.

● Slide one end of a short length of clear tube onto the bleed nipple.

● Put the other end of the tube into a plastic container that is big enough to hold the old brake fluid.

3 **Pull the brake lever** all the way back to the handlebar to remove some brake fluid.

● Tighten the bleed nipple.

● Make sure that all tools are at hand, since the next steps require you to be organized.

● Cover the surface below where you are working, since brake fluids can be corrosive. Use disposable mechanic's gloves to protect your hands.

6 **Replace the cover** of the brake fluid reservoir but be careful not to displace any brake fluid.

● Refit your wheels and pump the brake lever a few times to center the brake pads.

● Go for a flat test ride. If your brakes are not performing as they should, there may still be air in the system. Repeat Step 4 and make sure that everything is tight.

Roller-brake cable

All brake cables wear out, no matter how much time is spent maintaining them. Cables for roller brakes—sometimes called drum brakes—are no different. If the bike is equipped with roller brakes, the steps in this sequence show how to replace a cable when it is frayed or worn out. However, lubricating the brakes and replacing the internal parts are occasional jobs that are best left to the experts at a good bike shop.

If the rear inner tube is punctured, or it is necessary to take off the back tire to replace it, you need to know how to disconnect the rear brake in order to remove the back wheel. At the same time, you should know how to reconnect and adjust the brake after replacing the wheel. Once this is a familiar routine, it will also be possible to adjust the roller brakes for brake pad wear from time to time.

STEP LOCATOR

Parts of a roller brake

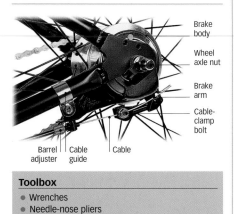

Brake body

Wheel axle nut

Brake arm

Cable-clamp bolt

Barrel adjuster | Cable guide | Cable

Toolbox

- Wrenches
- Needle-nose pliers

Replacing a roller-brake cable

1 **Push the brake–arm cradle** toward the front of the bike. This takes the tension from the cable so that you can unhook the cable-clamp bolt from the cradle and remove the old cable.

- Screw the barrel adjuster on the brake arm in or out to about half of its extent.

- Remove the wheel at this point if you need to replace the tire or inner tube.

4 **Tighten the cable–clamp bolt** while squeezing the cable slightly, as your helper keeps up the forward pull on the brake-arm cradle.

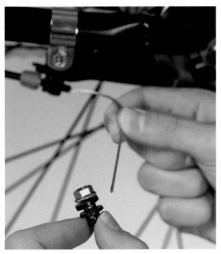

2 **Thread the greased cable** through the brake lever, then through the housing.

- Dribble a little oil into the housing.

- Make sure the housing is firmly located in the lever, then thread the cable through the barrel adjuster and seat the housing firmly into it.

- Thread the cable through the cable-clamp bolt.

3 **Pull the cable backward** with the needle-nose pliers while you push the brake-arm cradle forward and hook the clamp bolt into it.

- Bend the cable slightly behind the clamp bolt and ask someone to push the brake-arm cradle forward. Use your free hand to tighten up the bolt so the cable is nipped in place.

5 **Pull the brake lever hard** repeatedly (ten times) to bed in the brakes. The brakes may be a little tight, as if they are being applied gently, even when there is no pressure on the lever.

- Keep about ⅖in (15mm) of play in the brake lever before the brakes begin to bite.

6 **Screw in the barrel adjuster** a few turns until you achieve the ⅖in (15mm) of play in the brake lever.

- Pull in the lever after each turn in the adjuster to check when the brakes begin to bite.

TUNING YOUR

Suspension technology
has revolutionized
off-road riding. Accurate
adjustment of the front
fork and rear shock
allows uneven terrain to
be tackled safely and
confidently.

SUSPENSION

SUSPENSION FORKS

A suspension fork softens the blow of a bump on the road or trail. The fork must be checked for wear and lubricated regularly. The oil and springs should be changed either when they wear or to alter the characteristics of the fork.

How they work

The suspension fork on the front wheel absorbs the energy of a bump and prevents the force from reaching the rider. The fork's main spring, which can be trapped air or a metal coil, is compressed as the sliders move up the stanchions. Compression ends when the spring has absorbed the shock of the bump. At this point, the spring pushes the sliders back and the fork rebounds. Damping controls the speed of compression and rebound, usually by absorbing some of the energy of the bump with an air or oil damping mechanism. This creates friction, which slows down the fork's movements.

Reacting to bumps
Damping should prevent the fork from reaching the limits of its travel, but the fork should still be reactive enough to cope with every bump.

FRONT FORK COMPRESSION

Bunnyhopping gives a graphic demonstration of compression and rebound. As the rider picks up the front of the bike to clear the log, the fork rebounds because the rider's weight has been taken off the spring. On landing, the fork compresses as the spring absorbs the shock of the bike and rider landing.

Rebound

Pulling the handlebar upward *and moving the body backward lifts the front wheel so the front fork rebounds.*

Compression

Landing on the ground *returns the rider's weight to the bike's frame and compresses the front fork.*

AIR/OIL FORK

When a bump pushes up the sliders on this fork, a piston moves up the left stanchion, compressing the air. Once the bump has been absorbed, the air pushes the piston back and the fork rebounds. The damping mechanism in the right stanchion, which is full of oil, also moves up and down with the bump, controlling the speed of compression and rebound.

Fork crown
Turns the fork

Brake arch
Connects the two sliders

Seal
Keeps dirt out of fork's interior

Left stanchion
Contains the spring mechanism and piston

Right stanchion
Contains the damping mechanism

Air chamber
Contains air

Oil chamber
Contains oil

Damping mechanism
Moves up and down with slider

Piston
Moves up and down in response to bumps

Slider
Moves up and down on the stanchion

Shaft bolt
Fastens shaft to slider

Front suspension

A suspension fork works best if it has been set up to accommodate the rider's weight. When you sit on your bike, the amount the fork depresses, as the slider moves down the stanchion, is called the sag. As you ride, sag allows the fork to extend into the hollows in the ground, giving a smooth ride. To set the amount of sag, you can increase or decrease the amount of preload in the fork.

Damping controls the speed at which a fork works. To find out if a fork is working too fast, lean on the handlebar, then quickly lift up the front of the bike. If the suspension fork bangs back to its limit, its action is too quick and its rebound damping needs to be increased. Adjust the damping still further after a few rides. The best setup will let the fork absorb a hit and rebound quickly enough to be ready for the next.

STEP LOCATOR

Parts of a suspension fork

- Steerer
- Air valve
- Crown
- Stanchion
- Fork brace
- Brake boss
- Slider
- Dropout

Toolbox

- Shock pump ● Tie-wrap
- Tape measure

Setting sag

1 **Put a tie-wrap** around the stanchion of the unloaded fork and next to the top of the slider. Ideally, the sag should be about 25 percent of its available travel, though cross-country riders often prefer less and downhillers more.

3 **Get off the bike** and carefully measure the distance between the tie-wrap and the top of the slider.

● Express this measurement as a proportion of the fork's available travel. If the distance is 1in (25mm) on a 3⅛in (80mm) fork, the proportion is 32 percent. Check the owner's manual to find out the available travel of your bike.

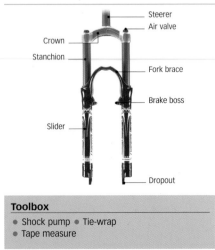

2 Sit on the bike, wearing your normal cycling clothes.

• Place both feet on the pedals. Either ask someone to hold you upright on the bike, or lean your elbow against a wall. The slider will travel up the stanchion, pushing the tie-wrap with it.

Fine-tuning the fork

1 Fine-tune the damping on some forks with an adjuster at the bottom of one of the fork blades. The two air chambers in this fork allow further refinements to damping.

• Pump air into the bottom chamber with a shock pump to change the spring characteristics.

• Change the size of a valve on the air piston to control air flow between chambers. This flow is called air-damping.

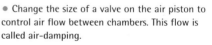

4 Increase the air in the chamber with a shock pump if the proportion of available travel is greater than 25 percent.

• Increase the spring preload with a coil/oil system (there is usually a dial at the top of the fork blade) or fit stronger springs.

• Release air, reduce the preload, or fit lighter springs if the proportion is less than 25 percent.

1 Make damping adjustments on some types of fork while riding the bike. The controls for these on-the-fly adjusters are usually marked "faster" and "slower" to indicate which direction to turn them in. It is also possible to lock out some forks. This means that you can stop their action if you are riding over a very smooth surface and do not need suspension.

Coil/oil fork

If the sag has been set up correctly (see pp.140–41) but the coil/oil fork keeps bottoming out—the fork reaches the full extent of its travel but the spring cannot compress any more—it will be necessary to fit heavier-duty springs. Conversely, if the fork only reacts to the bigger lumps and bumps, lighter springs should be fitted.

The method of changing springs is similar in most coil/oil forks, but check the manufacturer's manual to find the features of the fork on the bike in question. It may not be necessary to remove the fork blade from the fork crown; or a spring in both blades of the fork may need replacing; or one blade may incorporate the spring, while the other has the damping mechanism.

STEP LOCATOR

Parts of a coil/oil fork

- Steerer
- Fork crown
- Top cap
- Fork crown bolts
- Stanchion
- Fork brace
- Brake boss
- Slider
- Dropout

Toolbox

- Wrench ● Allen key multi-tool
- Flat screwdriver

Setting up a coil/oil fork

1 Remove the circle clip from around the rebound adjuster of the fork by prying it off with a flat screwdriver. Be very careful. Do not dig your screwdriver too far under the circle clip, but put it far enough under so that it does not slip. Keep your fingers away from the screwdriver to avoid injuring yourself if it slips.

4 Drop the new spring into the fork blade. Make sure that it sits correctly in the fork blade, then replace the top cap.

● Screw the top cap in with your fingers, then tighten it with a wrench.

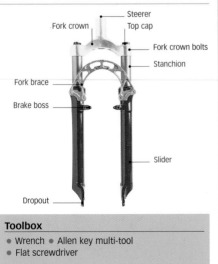

2 **Undo the retaining bolts** in the fork crown so that you can drop the blades out. There are usually four retaining bolts. Some fork crowns do not have them, in which case undo a cap bolt at the top of the fork blade to remove the springs.

3 **Start to remove the top cap** of the fork blade with a wrench on the wrench flats, then unscrew the cap the rest of the way out with your fingers.

● Note how the spring is sitting in the fork blade, then lift the spring out.

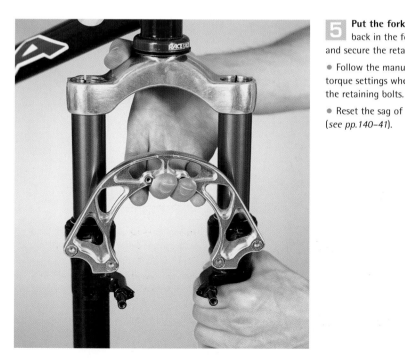

5 **Put the fork blades** back in the fork crown and secure the retaining bolts.

● Follow the manufacturer's torque settings when replacing the retaining bolts.

● Reset the sag of your forks (see pp.140–41).

Air/oil fork

Air/oil suspension forks usually have short travel and are popular with cross-country riders. Their spring medium is air, which makes them very light, and their mechanism is damped by oil.

Sometimes they have a negative spring working in the opposite direction of the main air spring. This helps to overcome the stiction (the sticky friction between two adjacent but motionless objects) which is inherent in air/oil suspension forks and is caused by their very tight seals.

Changing oil is necessary from time to time, as dirt in the system starts to cause excessive wear. If you have increased the damping on your fork and its action is still too fast, replacing the oil with a heavier one will slow it down. In the same way, lighter oil can help to speed it up.

STEP LOCATOR

Parts of an air/oil suspension fork

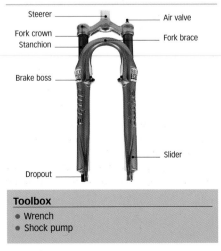

Steerer

Fork crown
Stanchion

Brake boss

Air valve

Fork brace

Slider

Dropout

Toolbox

- Wrench
- Shock pump

Changing oil

1 **Remove the cap** from the top of the stanchion without the Schrader air valve. This is the same kind of valve that is used on car tires. You can carry out this following sequence of steps with the fork still in the bike, although it is easier if someone helps you.

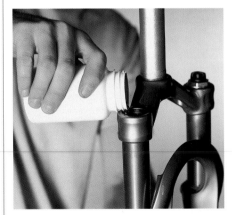

3 **Make sure that you hold** the fork blades absolutely vertical.

- Place a bowl under the fork to catch any spills. Carefully pour new oil into the stanchion until it is full and then replace the cap.

- Use a calibrated pouring vessel to ensure that you accurately measure the amount of oil, if the fork manufacturer specifies.

2 Pour the old oil out of the stanchion and into a plastic cup. This air/oil fork has an open-bath damping system, in which the damping rod moves up and down an open oil bath. The oil also lubricates the rest of the suspension system.

4 Put the cap back on top of the oil stanchion and tighten it.

● Set the sag again (*see pp.140–41*), pumping air in or letting it out to obtain the ideal sag.

● Tighten the Schrader valve if, after setting up the sag correctly, your fork works well at first, then starts to bottom out (the valve may be leaking). Use an automotive valve key.

5 Pump air in or let air out of a fork with negative air springs after you have replaced the oil with one of a different viscosity.

● Adjust the damping of the fork so that it works at the speed you require, then fine-tune its action with the negative spring.

● Pump air in to make the fork more active over small bumps. Let air out to make it less responsive.

Looking after suspension forks

Suspension forks soak up a lot of abuse because that is what they are designed to do. Although manufacturers do whatever they can to protect the inner workings, there are still some things you need to do to look after your forks.

Chief among them is cleaning. If you do not clean your forks regularly, dirt will wear down the seals at the top of the sliders and allow water to get into the inner workings and damage them. Worn seals will also allow oil to leak out, which affects the fork's performance.

Cleaning also gives you the opportunity to examine the forks for cracks and defects. You can also look for tell-tale signs of seal wear, such as the absence of a dirt ring on the stanchions after a ride—you should see this ring after every ride.

Another one of your regular jobs is to check the fork's settings. You can set the speed at which some forks work, along with other features. You need to check these settings have not been reset after a tough ride or after cleaning.

Do not use pressure hoses to clean suspension forks, since they can force water into the inner workings. You need to use a much gentler method of cleaning this part of your bike.

STEP LOCATOR

Toolbox
- Stiff-bristled brushes ● Sponge ● Oil
- Degreaser

Cleaning suspension forks

1 **Remove mud and dirt** with a dry, stiff-bristled brush. Remove the front wheel if there is a lot of mud on the fork, since it will make the job easier.

● Start at the top of the fork and brush downward. Take care not to scrub too hard around the fork seals.

● Use smaller brushes to get into hard-to-reach places on the fork.

4 **Apply light, Teflon-based lubricant** to the seals at the top of the sliders to keep them supple and help maintain their integrity.

● Apply the oil sparingly but make sure you spread it all around the circumference of both seals.

● Be careful not to spill oil on the tires of your bike. If you do spill any, wash it off immediately with hot, soapy water.

2 **Spray degreaser** all over the fork, especially on the stanchions, to remove the old oil and dirt—a mix that could corrode the seals on your fork.

● Again, start spraying degreaser from the top of the fork and work downward.

3 **Wipe the fork clean** with a clean sponge soaked in warm water. Wrap the sponge around the fork to ensure they get completely rinsed. Start from the top and work down.

● Remove the wheel so you can clean the lower part of the fork thoroughly.

● Examine the fork for cracks and defects while you perform this step.

5 **Pump the fork** up and down by pushing on the handlebars so that the seals become well coated.

● This is a good time to check for cracks on your handlebars and stem.

● Do not be tempted to alter the settings of the fork if it is hard to push. What matters is the way the fork feels when you ride.

6 **Check the settings dials** on your fork. Cleaning, especially when you use a stiff-bristled brush, can move the dials. Check that they are set where you want them for riding.

● Check the cable outers or hoses for wear over the crown of the fork.

● As a final step, turn your bike upside down for five minutes to help redistribute the oil inside the fork.

REAR SUSPENSION

The rear suspension absorbs the shock caused by a bump in the ground or rough terrain. A shock absorber must be kept clean and lubricated, and the bushings and frame mounts checked regularly for damage and wear.

How it works

The shock absorber of the rear suspension mirrors the specifications of the front fork in order to increase the rider's control of the bike. The rear triangle of the frame, which connects the rear wheel to the shock absorber, can move independently of the rest of the frame on bikes that are fitted with rear suspension.

Shock absorbers, or shocks, as they are also known, consist of a spring medium, either a coil or trapped air, and a shaft. The shaft is usually connected to a damping mechanism, which contains oil and controls the speed of the shock absorber's action.

Adjusting the shock
The shock absorber of the rear suspension can be adjusted to suit different kinds of terrain and gradients.

COMPRESSION OF THE SHOCK ABSORBER

When the back wheel hits a bump on the road or trail, the rear triangle moves up on its pivots, compressing the spring, which absorbs the shock.

As the spring pushes back on the rear triangle of the frame, the shock rebounds, pushing the rear wheel back ready for the next bump.

When riding over smooth ground *the rear shock absorber is in a neutral position.*

When riding over rough ground *the rear shock is in a compressed position to absorb bumps.*

AIR/OIL SHOCK ABSORBER ANATOMY

In an air/oil shock absorber, the spring mechanism is compressed air that is sealed inside an air sleeve. The damping mechanism in the shock body contains oil. When the bike hits a bump, the shock body travels up inside the air sleeve and compresses the trapped air. Once this air spring has absorbed the energy of the bump, the shock absorber begins to rebound and return to its original position. The shaft, which runs from the top of the air sleeve into the shock body, is connected to the damping device. Oil flowing through holes in the device slows the action of the shock absorber in compression and rebound as the shock body travels up and down.

Bushing
Attaches shock to frame

Air valve
Controls air pressure in the sleeve

Rebound adjuster
Changes speed of rebound

Shaft
Runs into shock body

Air sleeve
Contains compressed air

Shock body
Contains the damping device

Rear shock
Absorbs the force of a bump

Rear triangle
Transmits the force of a bump to the rear shock

Rear wheel
Moves up and down in response to bumps

Rear suspension

A good-quality, full-suspension bike should be designed with a rear shock absorber that complements and works with the suspension fork in the front. Air/oil forks are normally accompanied by an air/oil shock, and coil/oil systems are usually paired.

The first step in setting up a rear shock is to adjust its sag. Take into account the rider's weight, as with suspension forks (see pp.140–1), and then fine-tune its action by using damping and the shock's other functions after several rides on the bike.

One simple test to see if a rear shock is working in tune with the front fork is to press down on the middle of the bike while looking at how the fork and shock react. For general riding, each should depress about the same amount.

Add the frame mounts, to which a shock is attached, to the routine safety checks (see pp.32–3). Check the bushes that allow the shock to pivot—consult the manufacturer's guide for instructions.

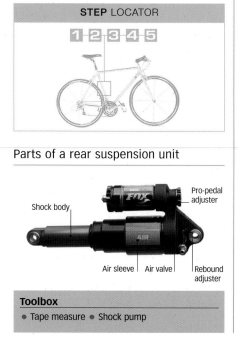

STEP LOCATOR

1 2 3 4 5

Parts of a rear suspension unit

Shock body

Pro-pedal adjuster

Air sleeve | Air valve | Rebound adjuster

Toolbox
- Tape measure ● Shock pump

Adjusting the sag

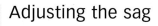

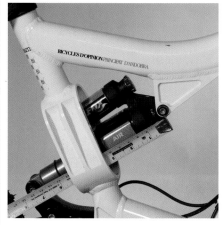

1 **Measure the centre-to-centre** distance between the shock-mounting bolts, with the bike unloaded.

● Familiarize yourself with the valves and various controls of your shock before going further.

3 **To achieve the proportion of sag** that your riding style requires, let air out or pump it in as needed, then take the second measurement again.

● If your bike has a coil/oil shock, increase or decrease the pre-load to achieve the measurement you want. The recommended range is only a guide.

2 **Sit on the bike** and ask someone to measure this distance again.

• Take both measurements and calculate the second as a percentage of the first. This will reveal the proportion of the shock's overall travel that is used as "sag." For general riding, the figure should be from a quarter, to a third.

• Cross-country racers tend to want stiffer shocks, so they sometimes go for a quarter or less.

• Downhill racers like their shocks to move a lot more. Their bikes often feel spongy to ride on the flat, but are really active when descending.

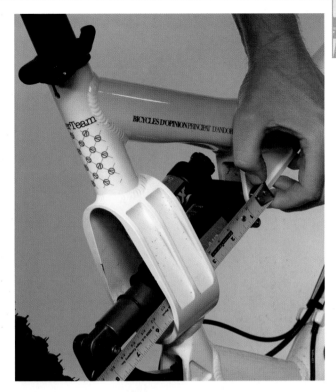

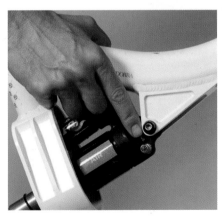

4 **Fine-tune the damping speed** of your shock with the rebound adjuster—if your bike has one.

• Turn the adjuster on an air/oil shock absorber but follow instructions on the shock to find out which way to turn.

• Do not set it too fast because this can upset the handling of the bike.

5 **Some shocks have additional** features. The pro-pedal system on this one allows you to control pedal-induced movement of the shock.

• Familiarize yourself with your shock's features by reading the instruction manual.

• Ride your bike across different terrains and see what happens when you vary the settings. Knowing all about your bike and the way you ride will help you get the best out of any trail situation.

Glossary

Terms in *italic* within an entry are defined under their own headings within the glossary.

ALLEN BOLT A threaded bolt with a hexagonal depression in the center of its head.

ALLEN KEY Hexagonal tool that fits *Allen bolts*.

BEARING A mechanism that usually consists of a number of ball bearings and circular channels, or races. It allows two metal surfaces to move freely while in contact.

BLOCK Cogs fitted to a *freewheel*.

BOSS Threaded metal fixture on a bicycle frame to which an item such as a bottle cage or a pannier rack is attached.

BOTTOM BRACKET Rotating unit that connects the *crankarms*.

BOTTOM OUT A term that describes the point when a *suspension* fork or shock absorber reaches the limit of its *travel*.

BRAKE–LEVER HOOD The body in which the brake lever sits, connecting it to the handlebar.

BRAKE TRAVEL The distance a brake lever moves before the brake pads engage the braking surface on the rim or hub of a wheel.

CABLE CRIMP A small metal cylinder that is closed at one end and fits over the cut ends of a cable to prevent fraying.

CASSETTE A collection of cogs that fit on the rear wheel's freehub.

CHAINRING A toothed ring attached to the *crankarms* that drives the chain and, in turn, the *cogs* and the rear wheel of a bicycle.

CHAINSTAY The frame tube joining the *bottom bracket* shell and rear *dropout*.

CRANKSET The assembly of *chainrings* and *crankarms*.

CLEAT A plastic or metal plate that fits on the sole of a cycling shoe and engages with a *clipless pedal* to hold the foot on the pedal.

CLIPLESS PEDAL A pedal with a mechanism to engage the *cleat* on the sole of a cycling shoe and hold it securely in place. Called clipless because they replaced pedals that had toe clips and straps.

COG A circular metal object with teeth that is turned by the chain. Combined with other cogs, it forms a *cassette* or *block*. Cogs are sometimes called "sprockets."

COMPRESSION The action of a *suspension* system when it absorbs an impact from the terrain. The term refers to the compression of the spring.

CRANKARM The lever that joins the pedals to the *chainrings* and transfers energy from the rider's legs to the *drivetrain* of the bike.

DAMPING The process that absorbs the energy of an impact transmitted through a *suspension* system. It controls the speed at which any form of suspension responds to uneven terrain.

DERAILLEUR Device that pushes the chain onto a larger or smaller *chainring* or *cog*. See also *Derailleur gears*.

DERAILLEUR GEARS A system that shifts the chain between *cogs* on the rear wheel (rear derailleur) and between *chainrings* attached to *crankarms* (front derailleur); it allows multiple gearing on bikes.

DOWN TUBE The frame tube that joins the *bottom-bracket* shell to the *head tube*.

DRIVETRAIN The assembly of pedals, *crankset*, chain, and *cogs* that drives the bike forward by converting the rider's leg power into wheel rotation.

DROPOUT A slotted plate at the end of the fork blades and stays, into which the axle of a wheel is attached.

EXPANDER BOLT A bolt that draws up a truncated cone or triangle of metal inside a metal tube in order to wedge the tube in place. Commonly found inside the stem of a threaded *headset*.

FREEHUB A mechanism, part of the hub, that allows the rear wheel to rotate while the pedals remain stationary.

FREEWHEEL A mechanism that does the same job as a *freehub* but can be screwed on or off the hub.

GEAR An expression of the *chainring* and *cog* combination, linked by the chain, that propels the bike.

GEAR-SHIFT LEVER The control mechanism, usually on the handlebar, used to initiate gear-shifts.

GRUB SCREW A headless, threaded bolt that has a single diameter throughout its length.

HEADSET The *bearing* unit that attaches the forks to a frame and allows them to turn. There are two varieties: threaded and threadless.

HEAD TUBE The frame tube through which the *steerer tube* runs.

HEXAGONAL BOLT OR NUT A threaded bolt with a hexagonal head, or a hexagonal nut that fits onto a threaded bolt.

HYDRAULIC A type of mechanical system that uses compressed fluid to move an object.

LOCKRING/LOCKNUT A ring or nut used to tighten onto a threaded object and lock it in place.

NEGATIVE SPRING A device that works against the main spring in a *suspension* system. In compression, for example, a negative spring works to extend the fork, helping to overcome the effects of *stiction*.

NIPPLE The piece of metal attached to the end of a cable that secures the cable in the control lever.

PLAY A term describing any looseness in mechanical parts.

QUICK-RELEASE MECHANISM A lever connected to a skewer that locks or releases a component from the frame.

REBOUND A term to describe the action of a *suspension* system after it absorbs an impact from the terrain. It refers to the extension of the system's spring.

SEAT POST A hollow tube that holds the saddle and is inserted into the *seat tube*.

SEAT STAY The frame tube joining the *bottom bracket* shell and rear *dropout*.

SEAT TUBE The frame tube that holds the *seat post*.

SIDEWALL Part of the tire between the *tread* and rim.

STEERER TUBE The tube that connects the fork to the *stem* and handlebar.

STEM The component that connects the handlebar to the *steerer tube*.

STICTION A term that combines the words "static" and "friction." It describes the tension between moving and static parts at rest, such as the seals and stanchions in a *suspension* fork.

STOPPER PIN The end of a cantilever or V-brake return spring that fits into a locating hole on the bike's brake-mounting *bosses*.

SUSPENSION An air/oil or coil/oil system that absorbs the bumps from a trail or road. The system is either integrated into the fork or connected to the rear wheel via a linkage.

THREADS The spiral grooves cut into metal that allow separate parts to be screwed or bolted together.

TOP TUBE The frame tube that joins the *seat tube* to the *head tube*.

TRAVEL A term that refers to the total distance a component moves in carrying out its purpose. For example, travel in a *suspension* fork is the total distance the fork has available to move in order to absorb a shock. Brake travel is the distance a brake lever must be pulled before the brakes fully contact the braking surface.

TREAD The central part of a tire that makes contact with the ground.

VISCOSITY A rating system for oils, which also refers to the weight. A light oil has low viscosity and moves more quickly than a heavy oil through a given *damping* mechanism. This results in a faster-acting *suspension* system or reduced damping.

WHEEL JIG A stand that holds a wheel so that its rim runs between two jaws. Used in truing a wheel after replacing a broken spoke.

Index

Acknowledgments

Author's acknowledgments

Pip Morgan and Richard Gilbert for their patient and diplomatic editorial work.

Ted Kinsey for designing everything so that the writing makes sense.

Dave Marsh of the Universal Cycle Centre for technical advice regarding road bikes.

Wayne Bennett of Don't Push It Mountain Bikes for advice regarding mountain bikes.

Tim Flooks of TF Tuned Shox for advice regarding suspension.

Gerard Brown for his excellent pictures and Guy Andrews for getting together the equipment we needed to show all the aspects of bike maintenance.

Jo Jackson and Keith and Barbara Oldfield for help when the author's computer broke down, twice.

Finally, all the bike companies who lent their equipment for our photoshoots.

Publisher's acknowledgments

Original edition produced by:
Senior Art Editor Kevin Ryan,
Art Editor Michael Duffy,
Managing Editor Adèle Hayward,
Managing Art Editor Karen Self,
Category Publisher Stephanie Jackson, **Art Director** Peter Luff,
DTP Designers Rajen Shah, Adam Shepherd, **Production Controller** Kevin Ward

Design: Janice English, Simon Murrell, Dawn Young

DTP Design: Gemma Casajuana

Photoshoot Art Director: Jo Grey

Picture Research: Carolyn Clerkin

Proofreading: Lynn Bresler

Illustrations: Kevin Jones and Matthew White at Kevin Jones Associates, Tim Loughead at Precision Illustration Ltd.

Additional photography: Jill and Steve Behr at Stockfile

Models: Jay Black, Chris Hopkins, James Millard, Simon Oon, Helen Rosser, Rochele Whyte

Cycling models: Hsu Minh Chung, Jamie Newell, Claire Paginton, Hannah Reynolds, Simon Richardson, Kelli Salone, Ross Tricker, Russell Williams

Accessory, component, and bicycle suppliers:
Ian Young at Moore Large for Schwinn BMX; Caroline Griffiths at Madison for Profile, Shimano, Finish Line, Park, Ridgeback, Cervelo, and Commencal; Ross Patterson and Jon Holdcroft at ATB sales for Electra and Marin bikes; Collette Clensy at Giant Bikes; Adrian at Pashley bicycles; Evans Cycles in Wandsworth and Milton Keynes; Cedric at Luciano Cycles, Clapham; Sam at Bikepark, Covent Garden; Richard at Apex Cycles, Clapham; Graham at SRAM; Shelley at Continental; Trek UK; Mike Cotty at Cannondale; Richard Pascoe of Ricci—Bike Chain; RJ Chicken; and Fisher Outdoor Leisure.

Picture credits

The publisher would like to thank the following for their kind permission to reproduce their photographs:

56–7: Stockfile/Steve Behr; 150: Fox Racing Shox.

All other images © DK Images.

For further information see **www.dkimages.com**

PLEASE NOTE

Bicycle maintenance is potentially hazardous. While the information in this book has been prepared with the reader's personal safety in mind, the reader may help to reduce the inherent risks involved by following these instructions precisely. The scope of this book allows for some, but not all, the potential hazards and risks to be explained to the reader. Therefore, the reader is advised to adopt a careful and cautious approach when following the instructions, and if in any doubt, to refer to a good bike shop or specialist.